KT-594-827

INSIGHT GUIDES

CORK

& SOUTHWEST IRELAND
Step by Step

APA PUBLICATIONS **L**

Part of the Langenscheidt Publishing Group

CONTENTS

Introduction

About this Book	4
Recommended Tours For...	6

Overview

Introduction	10
Food and Drink	14
Shopping	18
Entertainment	20
Sports and Outdoor Activities	22
Literary Heritage	24
History: Key Dates	26

Walks and Tours

1. Cork City	30
2. Cork Harbour and East Cork	36
3. Blarney Castle and the Lee Valley	42
4. Blackwater Valley and North Cork	46
5. Kinsale and Roaringwater Bay	50
6. Bantry Bay	56
7. The Ring of Beara	60
8. Killarney	64
9. The Ring of Kerry	68
10. The Dingle Peninsula	73
11. Tralee and North Kerry	77
12. Bunratty, Limerick and Adare	80

Directory

A–Z	86
Accommodation	96
Restaurants	102

Credits and Index

Picture Credits	108
Index	109

ABOUT THIS BOOK

This *Step by Step Guide* has been produced by the editors of Insight Guides, whose books have set the standard for visual travel guides since 1970. With top-quality photography and authoritative recommendations, this guidebook brings you the very best of Cork and southwest Ireland in a series of 12 tailor-made tours.

WALKS AND TOURS

The tours in the book provide something to suit all budgets, tastes and trip lengths. As well as covering the region's spect-cular landscapes and many classic attractions, the routes track lesser-known sights and up-and-coming areas. The tours embrace a range of interests, so whether you are an art fan, a gourmet, a lover of flora or have kids to entertain, you will find an option to suit.

We recommend that you read the whole of a tour before setting out. This should help you to familiarise yourself with the route and enable you to plan where to stop for refreshments – options for this are shown in the 'Food and Drink' boxes, rec-ognisable by the knife-and-fork sign, on most pages.

For our pick of the tours by theme, consult Recommended Tours For... *(see p.6–7).*

OVERVIEW

The tours are set in context by this introductory section, giving an overview of the region to set the scene, plus background information on food and drink, shopping, entertainment, outdoor activities and literary heritage. Also included is a succinct history timeline, which highlights the key events that have shaped Cork and southwest Ireland over the centuries.

DIRECTORY

Also supporting the tours is a Directory chapter, comprising a user-friendly, clearly organised A–Z of practical information, our pick of where to stay while you are in the region and select restaurant listings; these eateries complement the more low-key cafés and restaurants that feature within the tours and are intended to offer a wider choice for evening dining.

Above: Cork highlights include traditional pubs, horse riding across quiet beaches and countryside, pretty meadows, isolated islands and peninsulas and historic monuments such as the Drombeg Stone Circle *(see p.53)*.

The Author

Alannah Hopkin grew up in London and has lived in Kinsale since 1982, working as a writer on travel and the arts, and frequently contributing to Insight's Irish titles. Her latest travel book is *Eating Scenery: West Cork: the People and the Place* (Cork, 2008), which looks at the changes in one part of rural southwest Ireland over the past 30 years. She still gets excited about exploring her adopted home and showing friends around. Once they have got over the amazing scenery and the slower pace of life, what impresses her visitors most is the genuine friendliness they meet at every turn.

Margin Tips
Shopping tips, historical facts, handy hints and information on activities help visitors to make the most of their time in Cork and the southwest.

Feature Boxes
Notable topics are highlighted in these special boxes.

Key Facts Box
This box gives details of the distance covered on the tour, plus an estimate of how long it should take. It also states where the route starts and finishes, and gives key travel information such as which days are best to do the route or handy transport tips.

Footers
Look here for the tour name, a map reference and the main attraction on the double-page.

Route Map
Detailed cartography shows the tour clearly plotted with numbered dots. For more detailed mapping, see the pull-out map slotted inside the back cover.

Food and Drink
Recommendations of where to stop for refreshment are given in these boxes. The numbers prior to each restaurant/café name link to references in the main text. Restaurants in the Food and Drink boxes are plotted on the maps. The abbreviations 'B', 'L', 'AT' and 'D' stand for breakfast, lunch, afternoon tea and dinner, respectively.

The € signs at the end of each entry reflect the approximate cost of a two-course meal for one, not including drinks. These should be seen as a guide only. Price ranges, also quoted on the inside back flap for easy reference, are:

€€€€	38 euros and above
€€€	28–38 euros
€€	20–28 euros
€	20 euros and below

ARCHAEOLOGY

Connect with prehistoric man at Drombeg Stone Circle (tour 5). Appreciate the heft of Labbacallee Wedge Tomb, 4,000 years on site (tour 4). Follow in the footsteps of the early Christian monks on the rocky slopes of Skellig Michael (tour 9).

RECOMMENDED TOURS FOR...

BEACHES

Walk for kilometres along lonely Banna Strand, then stretch out in the dunes (tour 11). Reconnect with your inner child among the rock pools at Derrynane (tour 9). Simmer in hot seawater infused with freshly picked seaweed in Ballybunion's beachside bathhouse (tour 11).

CASTLES

Climb to the top of Blarney Castle to gauge the size of it (tour 3). Wander the grassy paths of star-shaped Charles Fort on Kinsale Harbour (tour 5). View the mighty River Shannon from the bastion at King John's Castle, Limerick (tour 12).

CHILDREN

Roam free with giraffes and wallabies at Fota Wildlife Park (tour 2). Take a tour of Tralee in the year 1450, including its smells, at Kerry County Museum (tour 11). Walk among the free-range hens in the village streets of Bunratty Folk Park (tour 12).

FESTIVALS

The city swings, as visitors flock to the Cork Jazz Festival in late October (tour 1). Hear international virtuosos perform at Bantry House during the West Cork Chamber Music Festival (tour 6). Take a workshop at Listowel Writers' Week, and mingle with the literati in the quaint Kerry town (tour 11).

FINE FOOD

Revel in traditional and artisan foods in Cork's English Market (tour 1). Take a course at the Ballymaloe Cookery School; it could change your life (tour 2). Eat out in Kinsale (tour 5) and Kenmare (tour 9), and decide which is the fine food capital of Ireland.

GARDENERS

A riverside Robinsonian garden, with giant foliage plants, Annes Grove Garden is both witty and romantic (tour 4). Some of the tallest tree ferns in Europe thrive at Glanleam Gardens on Valentia (tour 9). Take a boat to visit Illnacullin near Glengarriff, and enjoy the Happy Valley of azaleas.

GREAT VIEWS

See the wide sweep of Bantry Bay and the mountains beyond from the tiny Goat's Path (tour 6). Watch the surf crash on to the rocky headlands of Dingle's Slea Head (tour 10). Drive the crazy switchback road between Allihies and Eyeries (tour 7).

IRISH HOSPITALITY

Experience an older Ireland among the trawlermen in McCarthy's Bar, Castletownbere (tour 7). While away a rainy day playing darts at The Spaniard (tour 5). The Dunraven Arms is a luxury hotel, but remains a village inn at heart (tour 12).

WALKERS

Rise to the challenge of walking through Killarney's Gap of Dunloe (tour 8). Sea views, sheep, turf and rock abound on the long-distance Beara Way (tour 7). Enjoy a quiet riverside stroll in picturesque Adare (tour 12).

OVERVIEW

An overview of the geography, customs and culture of Cork and southwest Ireland, plus illuminating background information on food and drink, shopping, entertainment, sports and outdoor activities, literary heritage and history.

INTRODUCTION   10
FOOD AND DRINK   14
SHOPPING   18
ENTERTAINMENT   20
SPORTS AND OUTDOOR ACTIVITIES   22
LITERARY HERITAGE   24
HISTORY: KEY DATES   26

INTRODUCTION

The rolling countryside of southwest Ireland leads to wild seascapes and rocky shorelines, with pockets of subtropical vegetation. Hospitality is an ingrained tradition, part of the way of life of a small, mainly rural, population.

Southwest Ireland is the furthest part of the country from the capital, Dublin, and so least influenced by it. Of the area's three counties (Cork, Kerry and Limerick), Kerry has such an independent attitude that its nickname is 'The Kingdom', while Cork is known as the 'Rebel County'. As you venture further south and west, scantily inhabited hills lead to a rugged Atlantic coast, where the legacy of the area's Celtic and Gaelic past persists. The growth of tourism coincided with the decline of the small farm, to the benefit of both sectors, as evidenced in the network of waymarked walking routes, and the revival of artisan foods.

GEOGRAPHY
AND LAYOUT

Southwest Ireland is that area to the south and west of a line drawn from Lismore on the Blackwater River in the east to Bunratty on the Shannon Estuary in the west. The central plain is bisected by the Blackwater River (Ireland's second-longest river after the Shannon) and the River Lee.

Cork City is built on a series of islands, where the Lee has been chan-nelled to the sea. Between Cork and Skibbereen the south-facing coast has a series of pretty fishing villages. The extreme west of the region has the most dramatic seascapes, on peninsulas that jut out into the Atlantic, benefiting from the Gulf Stream. The northernmost Kerry coast is on the River Shannon's long estuary.

Getting Around

The tours in this book begin with a day-long walk around Cork City, which can be extended to the university campus. A short drive to the east, Cobh, a Victorian seaport and the main embarkation point for Ireland's emigrants, has a fascinating history. Midleton boasts Ireland's largest whiskey distillery, while Ballymaloe House is famous for the revival of Irish cookery. The next two drives explore the two river valleys, the Lee and the Blackwater, visiting some charming, less-frequented spots.

The tours then work around the coast to the west. Starting with a walking tour of Kinsale, also known as the 'gourmet capital of Ireland', the tour goes through a series of attractive fishing villages. Circular drives around

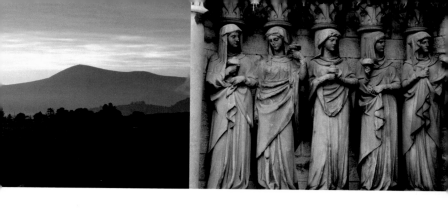

the four peninsulas start with the smallest, the Sheep's Head on Bantry Bay. The Beara Peninsula is the least developed, with breathtaking coastal scenery. Inland is Killarney, where our tour will enable you to enjoy the scenery while avoiding the crowds. The Ring of Kerry's famous scenic drive contrasts the rugged north-facing coast with the subtropical vegetation of the Kenmare River. Slea Head on the Dingle Penin-sula has dramatic cliffs dotted with archaeological remains. From Tralee, the next tour drives around the coast of Tralee Bay, returning to Listowel. The final tour starts at Bunratty, near

to Shannon Airport, and works its way south through Limerick City and the village of Adare.

Note that public transport is a weak point in this region, with the only com-fortable way to visit it being by car.

HISTORY AND ARCHITECTURE

The early settlers left their marks all over the area, from megalithic tombs in the Blackwater Valley, to the mys-terious stone circles of west Cork and Kerry. The monastery built offshore on the rocky slopes of Skellig Michael, and Gallarus Oratory near Dingle,

Above from far left: hiking on the island of Skellig; Killarney, Ring of Kerry; statues adorning Corks St Fin Barre's Cathedral.

Above: the ruins of Ardfert Abbey; colourful houses in Cork.

Left: Cork's Nano Nagle Bridge, with the National Monument to the left.

Population Density

The economic depression of the mid-20th century hit the southwest especially hard, with many villages being so depleted by emigration that there were not enough children to form a football team. Nowadays, the average population density for southwest Ireland has been calculated at 34 people per sq km, (11 per sq mile), falling to 25 per sq km (8 per sq mile) on Beara.

were built by Irish monks in the 6th to the 9th centuries.

The Anglo-Normans arrived in 1169, and quickly intermarried with the native families. They took over and added to the massive tower houses built by the native chieftains, and also had a strong influence on Irish church architecture, endowing monks from continental orders who brought the architecture of mainland Europe with them. Their heritage today often includes hauntingly beautiful ruins in secluded spots, including Bridgewater Priory in the Blackwater Valley, Innisfallen Island in Killarney and Ardfert Cathedral in north Kerry.

When Queen Elizabeth I decided to bring unruly Catholic Cork to order, one who resisted ceding his castle to the Crown was the owner of Blarney Castle. The Spanish landed at Kinsale in 1601 to support the Irish Catholics against the English, but were resoundingly defeated at the Battle of Kinsale. The star-shaped Charles Fort was built to defend Kinsale harbour against further foreign invasions.

From Famine to Feast

Sir Walter Raleigh is credited with bringing the potato to Ireland. It rapidly became the staple diet of the poorest people, who were devastated by the failure of the potato crop between 1845 and 1850. The Beara and Iveragh peninsulas lost three-quarters of their population, leaving

vast tracts of land uninhabited. There followed a century of political unrest and economic depression. Only in the 1980s did the population of rural Cork and Kerry start to grow again.

CLIMATE

The southwest of Ireland has a mild maritime climate. July is the warmest month with temperatures averaging 14–15°C (57–9°F), and February is the coldest with averages of 4–5°C (39–41°F). Between December and March the days are short, with the sun setting at around 4.30pm, and rain can be persistent. In contrast, summer evenings are long, with daylight until 10pm or later. July and August are traditionally the time for the Irish summer, but it doesn't always arrive. The best times to visit are late spring and early autumn: May to June, and September to October.

POPULATION

Rural southwest Ireland has gone from being a static traditional community to a varied, multicultural one. As the economy started to boom, people who had moved abroad returned home with their children. Others moved to the area to live in an unpolluted environment with a less pressured lifestyle, while younger people from Eastern Europe, many from a rural Catholic background, headed there

after the expansion of the European Union (EU) in 2004. The development of tourism, and the availability of cheap flights, have also helped to revitalise the area.

LOCAL CUSTOMS

The features that attracted incomers to the southwest – friendliness, a strong sense of community and a slower pace of life – have, by and large, survived. Drivers still habitually salute each other when passing on remote roads, and strangers still exchange pleasantries when passing on foot. It is courtesy to ask questions of visitors, such as where you come from and whether you are enjoying your holiday. Try to slow down enough to take part in these exchanges; they will greatly enhance your visit.

POLITICS AND ECONOMICS

Politically the southwest is a traditional area, with families voting the way their forefathers voted. The Republic's two main parties have their origins in Ireland's Civil War (1922–3), which was fought intensively in the Cork hinterland. Fianna Fáil (Warriors of Ireland) draws its support from small farmers, and entrepreneurs (including publicans), while Fine Gael (Tribes of Ireland) is supported by larger-scale farmers and the professional classes.

Left and right wing mean very little in Irish politics: tribal loyalty is all. While there is an active Green Party in the southwest, it has had very little impact on traditional patterns of voting.

Economics

Because the economic boom was less intensive in this area, so the bust has been less of a trauma. While there are some empty estates and office blocks, it is nothing like as dramatic as in other parts of Ireland. In fact the recession, with its emphasis on holidaying at home, has given a boost to the tourism sector in the southwest. Prices have been slashed, and special offers abound, making this a very good time to visit.

A WARM WELCOME

Nobody goes to southwest Ireland for the weather, and the prices are not cheap, but the region continues to attract visitors, many of them keen to sample the unspoilt wilderness areas by walking or cycling. The people have retained their natural courtesy in spite of increasing visitor numbers. In a world of increasing homogeneity, the southwest of Ireland still manages to be distinctively different, capable of surprising even the most jaded visitor, usually by an unsolicited act of kindness. This is perhaps the last place in Europe where slow cars and trucks voluntarily pull over to the hard shoulder to let the faster car past.

Above from far left: barrels of Jameson's Irish Whiskey; cows on the Ring of Kerry; fishing boats at sea.

Above: the easy way to sightsee; pretty rural cottage.

FOOD AND DRINK

The southwest has been setting the pace in Ireland's culinary revolution, with a new generation of chefs using the abundant fresh local produce to create an exciting dining experience at all price levels.

Traditionally the eating-out scene in southwest Ireland was dominated by hotel restaurants, and these were not particularly edifying places. Bread and potatoes accompanied the main meal, usually consisting of a hearty portion of roast meat, or fish on Fridays. The meat was overcooked, the vegetables were boiled to a pulp, and salads were a rare summer treat.

However, in only one generation Irish cooking has changed beyond all recognition. There is a new awareness of the high quality of the raw materials available to chefs in the form of grass-fed beef and lamb, fresh seafood from the Atlantic, abundant dairy produce and home-grown vegetables and salads. The southwest has pioneered the revival of Irish artisan foods, in particular farmhouse cheese and home-baked bread.

Because of the low rents available in the region during the 1980s, the southwest was also a pioneer of the 'front parlour' restaurant, which saw ambitious young chefs opening their own restaurant on a shoestring, turning the biggest room in the house or shop into a dining room, to the great delight of locals and visitors alike.

LOCAL CUISINE

The food revolution that has taken place in the southwest over the past 30 years has as much to do with a return to the region's roots as it has with innovation. Southwest Ireland has always produced excellent beef, lamb and pork, and up until the 1960s it did so without the help of chemicals. Butter was the region's most famous export. Hens, ducks, geese and turkeys were naturally free-range, left to forage in the farmyard, while fish came in fresh from the Atlantic, direct from fishing boats. Shellfish were there for the taking in summer, and game (pheasant, woodcock, wild duck, snipe, venison) in the winter. Many rural households baked soda bread, made without yeast or any additives, daily.

The Ballymaloe Factor

The name that always comes to the fore when looking at the revival of Irish cuisine is that of Myrtle Allen, the doyenne of Ballymaloe House. When she opened a restaurant in the front room of her elegant period farmhouse, she served the sort of food that she would give her family, pre-

pared with simplicity and respect for its natural flavours. Myrtle, still going strong in her 80s, was one of the people who introduced the Slow Food Movement, which chimes so neatly with her philosophy, to Ireland. In 1983, her daughter-in-law, Darina Allen, set up the Ballymaloe Cookery School to pass on the message to a generation eager to make a living in the restaurant and bar-food business, or simply to cook better for their family.

The English Market

Another historic factor encouraging the new cuisine and the production of traditional artisan foods is Cork's large indoor market, the English Market. Here the traditional world of pork butchers, poultry merchants, fishmongers, bakers and greengrocers met the new world of farmhouse cheese makers, continental charcuterie butchers, and importers of olives and olive products, pasta, spices and other ingredients from overseas. Several Cork restaurants, including the market's own Farmgate, make a point of sourcing all their raw materials in the market.

Sourcing the Menu

Irish chefs are trained in the classic tradition, and most go abroad for a few years, and bring back culinary influences from their travels – generally Mediterranean. Chefs in the

Above from far left: artisan bread; olives and other Mediterranean appetisers at Cork city's English Market.

Above: eggs and potatoes, staple food.

Left: simple but irresistible: bread, creamy Kerry butter and a pint of Guinness.

southwest work closely with artisan food producers, who use traditional methods to smoke fish and make charcuterie and farmhouse cheeses. Many restaurants grow their own salads and herbs, or have an arrangement with a local grower.

All meat in Ireland is traceable back to the farm; the flavour of locally reared and butchered meat is excellent. The freshness of local fish and shellfish, served direct from the boat, is striking too. Suppliers are often mentioned on the menu, to reassure patrons that they are being served the best possible, locally sourced produce. Sample Frank Hederman's smoked salmon on a slice of Declan Ryan's wholemeal sourdough, for example, and you will notice the difference, and want to do so again.

Traditional Favourites

The fondness for the potato continues to be a national characteristic. In popular family restaurants the humble 'spud' will often be served in three different ways – mashed, chipped and dauphinoise, for example. Irish people like a steak when they eat out, and it will be found on most menus. Bread has become a star turn, with many places baking a selection daily. Fish and chips are also perennial favourites, traditionally eaten outdoors as a takeaway, but now served even in the most up-market restaurants. Fish has become popular, and is often on

menus as 'seafood chowder', a loosely used term, which varies greatly from one place to another, but is usually delicious. Mussels, which were rarely seen on a menu in the past, are also now a firm favourite, whether steamed with *frites*, or grilled in the shell with garlic breadcrumbs.

WHERE TO EAT

Fine Dining

Some of the best restaurants in the southwest are still to be found in hotels, such as Longueville House near Mallow, or the Park Hotel Kenmare. Such establishments also usually serve bar food at lunch, which offers the traveller on a budget a chance to sample good food in impressively luxurious surroundings.

Front Parlour Restaurants

These small, idiosyncratic establishments are the most typical of the southwest, even in the cities. Cork's famous vegetarian restaurant, Café Paradiso, is in this category, being a simply converted shop, albeit serving stunningly imaginative food. Out of the Blue, Dingle's leading seafood restaurant, is not even an ex-front parlour: it is, quite frankly, a tin shed, but the food is the draw, not the decor. So do not judge the book by its cover: these small restaurants, run by passionate owner-chefs, pack a big punch when it comes to cuisine.

Bistros, Wine Bars and Brasseries

The Irish use these terms indiscriminately, to indicate an informal, fun place without tablecloths. A high rate of VAT and high overheads make it very difficult to run a stylish, inexpensive establishment, but people do try. Casino House near Kinsale offers outstanding bistro-style food in a stylishly converted farmhouse, while Max's Wine Bar in Kinsale, with its talented French owner-chef, is a serious restaurant by most standards, not a wine bar.

Pubs

Since the introduction of the smoking ban and drink-driving laws, pubs have had to diversify. Nearly everywhere now serves tea and coffee, and espresso machines are commonplace in cities and fashionable resorts. More are serving food, with a short all-day menu, and daily specials at lunch and in the evening. The best, like Jim Edwards in Kinsale, have effectively turned into restaurants. The heartiest option for those who (like many Irish people) eat their main meal at midday is a 'carvery lunch' – roast meat carved at a self-service counter, served with potatoes and vegetables.

DRINKS

Irish pubs are expensive. A pint of beer in Cork city can set you back about €5 (compared to about €3.80 in a rural pub), and a soft drink can cost €3.50. Wine by the glass goes from €4.50–6 for the house variety, upwards. Try to be philosophical: it is not just the drink you are paying for, it is the real Irish pub experience. With any luck you will also get some free music, or some witty conversation.

Irish Stout

Irish pubs sell the usual range of beer and lager, in pints and half pints, but the one that every visitor has to try is stout, a strongish black beer with a creamy white head.

Murphy's is the Cork product, but the most famous stout is Guinness. Great care is taken in serving it: about half a glass is poured and left to 'settle' for several minutes, then topped with the trade-mark creamy head. The smooth taste bears no relation to that of the Guinness served in Britain or America.

Irish Whiskey

It's spelt differently from Scotch 'whisky', and tastes different too, as it is distilled from a mixture of malted and unmalted barley. The most popular brands are Bushmills, Jameson and Paddy. The fine old single malts are generally taken neat or with a splash of water as a *digestif*. Irish whiskey is also used in Irish coffee, a hot, sweet coffee spiked with whiskey and topped with cream, an indulgent way to end a meal.

Above from far left: traditional pub; pulling that perfect pint; colourful café sign.

Above: the drinks of choice to many in the region.

Hot Whiskey

If you have been too long in the cold outdoors, there is no better cure than a hot whiskey, ideally sipped in front of an open fire. The bartender should dissolve a teaspoon of sugar in about 3cm (1in) of boiling water, with a slice of lemon studded with cloves, and, of course, a measure of whiskey. Add more hot water to taste, and feel the warmth spreading to the very core of your being.

SHOPPING

In this part of Ireland, particularly outside the main city centres, there is a proliferation of small art and craft boutiques, where you are encouraged to linger. Homegrown Irish products (woollen goods, crystal, etc) don't come cheap, with many items aimed at the tourist market and priced accordingly.

While nobody could claim that the southwest is a shopper's paradise, few visitors leave without at least buying a sweater, a tweed cap or a ceramic puffin. Cork city and Limerick are the only places with any real density of shops. The resorts around the coast, especially Kinsale, Kenmare and Dingle, have some interesting designer shops and galleries, and all have good bookshops. You can even find attractive items in the more obviously tourist-orientated shops in Blarney, Glengarriff and Killarney.

SHOPPING AREAS

Cork City

Cork city's shopping area centres on St Patrick Street. The most expensive department store is Brown Thomas, where womenswear (including Irish designer labels) is on the first floor. They also stock a good selection of Irish Crystal, including Waterford. To the south of St Patrick Street, Oliver Plunkett Street has women's fashion boutiques, while to the north, in the Paul Street area, the mood is funkier, with vintage clothing and high fashion. To the north of the River Lee on MacCurtain Street there is a cluster of interior design shops, selling both antique and modern goods.

Limerick

Limerick also has a main shopping street called Patrick Street, and a branch of Brown Thomas, although both are quite a bit smaller than those in Cork. The liveliest part of Limerick's shopping scene is Cruises Street, near the junction of Patrick and William streets.

Blarney, Glengarriff and Killarney

Blarney Woollen Mills, Avoca, the Kilkenny Shop and Quill's Woollen Market will become familiar names, with branches all around the southwest. But these shops are not just for the tourist: many Irish people shop here too, for rainwear, knitwear and designer clothes (including linen shirts). Look out for the craft shop Bricin on Killarney's main street, and don't miss contemporary art by local artists at the Frank Lewis Gallery in a pedestrian alley near the General Post Office.

Farmers' Markets

These weekly outdoor markets at which producers sell directly to the public have been a great addition to the shopping scene in the southwest. They are ideal for picnic food, offering farmhouse cheese, bread, charcuterie and pâté, and for gifts, such as jams, handmade chocolates, chutneys and sauces. Schull's market, Sundays from about noon, also sells crafts, while you will find a huge variety of produce at Bantry's Friday-morning market. See www.bordbia.ie.

JEWELLERS

Kinsale, Kenmare and Dingle

These are places to go and browse on a rainy day, their narrow streets packed with appealing, often quirky, boutiques and art galleries. Prices can be hefty, especially in one-off ceramics, silverware and uncut lead crystal, but look on it as an investment.

WHAT TO BUY

Crystal

Heavy lead crystal is definitely in the heirloom category, but sometimes it is hard to resist a perfectly shaped vase or a set of six glasses. Kinsale Crystal is run by a former worker at Waterford Crystal, and has some classic pieces.

Art, Ceramics and Craft Wares

The boom years led to a veritable explosion in the Irish art market, and the taste for buying original art seems to have survived the recession. Kinsale's Keane on Ceramics is a gallery representing most of Ireland's leading ceramic artists. Look out for members of the West Cork Craft Guild at shops in Clonakilty and Schull. Louis Mulcahy, whose pottery is at Clogher Strand on the Dingle Peninsula, makes beautiful lamps and tableware, and has a good selection of seconds.

Craft items made in the southwest include wood-turning, traditional willow basketry, handmade candles, photography, batiks, silver and gold jewellery and cutlery.

Knitwear

Be sure you know the difference between hand-knitted and hand-loomed – the latter is the lesser form, actually handmade by machine, but more affordable. Either one will probably last a lifetime.

Food

Consider taking home a side of smoked salmon, vacuum packed, from one of the region's fine smokeries, or a handmade farmhouse cheese: Durrus, Milleens and Gubbeen are among the best. (Note that dairy goods and meat must bear the EU health mark stamp and be appropriately packaged if they are to be taken through customs.) Single malt whiskey, or even regular Irish whiskey, is usually a welcome gift.

Above from far left: bookshop in Kinsale; jewellers in Cork.

Above: quality woollen goods.

Opening Times
In Cork city shops open from 9am to 6pm, with late-night opening until 8pm on Thursdays. In the smaller towns grocery shops open from 8.30am or 9am until 9pm or later. Many smaller shops close for lunch from 1–2pm.

Left: shopping in Cork.

ENTERTAINMENT

Most entertainment in the southwest takes place on the pub scene, where it is usually free, or staged as part of a programme of festivals, which is when the local drama scene is at its liveliest.

While the both Cork and Limerick have the sort of cultural life you would expect in university cities, outside the pub scene most entertainment in the area is seasonal and designed to attract visitors.

OPERA AND THEATRE

Cork Opera House (Emmet Place; tel: 021-427 0022; www.corkoperahouse.ie) is the main theatre in the region, and hosts touring productions by companies from Ireland and abroad, as well as producing some of its own shows.

The **Everyman Palace Theatre** (MacCurtain Street; tel: 021-450 1673; www.everymanpalace.com), also in Cork, is a refurbished Victorian music hall, which hosts visiting productions, chiefly mainstream theatre.

DANCE

Tralee's **Siamsa Tire** (Godfrey Place, Town Park; tel: 066-712 3055; www.siamsatire.com) is Ireland's National Folk Theatre, and presents lively, dance-based versions of traditional Irish myths and legends.

Irish dance features in Irish cabaret at Bunratty Castle (Bunratty, Co. Limerick; tel: 061-361511; www.shannonheritgae.com), and there are occasional Riverdance-style touring productions at the region's larger venues, including the **Irish National Event Centre** (INEC) at the Gleneagles Hotel, Killarney (Gleneagles Hotel, Muckross Road; tel: 064-667 1555; www.ince.ie).

Even more enjoyable are set-dancing sessions, like barn or square dances. These take place in pubs and community halls, and are more common in County Killarney and rural County Kerry than in County Cork. Newcomers are usually welcomed and taught a few steps.

MUSIC

For traditional music, the pub is the best place to go. A gathering of musicians on an informal, unpaid basis is known as a *seisiún* (session), and creates its own momentum, as musicians improvise and take flight. Dingle's pubs have spontaneous sessions most nights. The two most famous traditional music pubs in Dingle are An Droicead Beag (The Small Bridge),

Above: the musical traditional is going strong in Ireland.

Above from far left:
Cork Opera House;
jazz festival in Cork;
pubs often have
music nights.

on Main Street, and O'Flaherty's, Holyground. Elsewhere, publicans employ musicians to entertain their customers from about 10pm, usually for free. There is a tradition unique to Killarney of the singing pub, where the MC encourages everyone to volunteer a solo or sing along with the musicians. The Laurels in Main Street and Danny Mann in New Street have ballad sessions from 9pm every night.

Classical Music

There are regular concerts by both local and visiting musicians at the **Cork School of Music** (Union Quay, Cork; tel: 021-480 7310). The University of Limerick (www.ul.ie) has a fine concert hall. Elsewhere in the region churches are often used for classical concerts. **West Cork Music** (13 Glengarriff Road, Bantry; tel: 027-52797; www.westcorkmusic.ie) has a year-round schedule of concerts in local churches and Bantry House.

Rock and Pop

Cork, Limerick, Killarney and Tralee have lively club scenes, with events advertised in the local press. Most small towns have at least one late-night pub or club with a DJ or a local band, or both, operating from Thursday to Sunday nights. The biggest venue in the region for visiting big-name acts is the INEC *(see opposite)*. Thomond Park Rugby Stadium in Limerick is also used for big-name acts.

Festivals

Cork is known as the festival city, with a packed annual calendar that starts in mid-March with a two-day St Patrick's Day festival *(see p.90)*, and ends in late October with the mammoth Cork Jazz Festival. Other big events are the Choral Festival in May, the Film Festival in September and, best of all, June's Midsummer Festival, which has theatre, cabaret, comedy and music. Much of the festivals' entertainment is free, and takes place on the streets and in the city's pubs. For details of Cork's festival calendar see www.disc-erireland.com. A Taste of Baltimore and Wooden Boat festival (www.baltimorewoodenboatfestival.com) opens the regatta season in late May, and combines stalls of local artisan food with the racing of locally built traditional wooden boats. Listowel Writers' Week (www.writersweek.ie) on the first week in June is an intimate occasion, at which would-be writers rub shoulders with big names. It is more than matched by the West Cork Literary Festival (www.westcorkliteraryfestival.ie) in Bantry in early July, where the emphasis is more international. This is preceded by the West Cork Chamber Music Festival (www.westcorkmusic.ie), held in the library of Bantry House. Kinsale Arts Week (www.kinsaleartsweek.com) in mid-July features open-air concerts in Charles Fort, and has a packed 10-day schedule of events. Free concerts take place daily in the town square, and there are tours of local artists' studios. Killorglin's Puck Fair (www.puckfair.ie) in August is a traditional fair with horse-trading alongside the festivities.

SPORTS AND OUTDOOR ACTIVITIES

Southwest Ireland has long been a destination for lovers of the outdoors. Initially attracting golfers and anglers, its accessible wilderness areas now lure walkers, climbers and cyclists, and its beaches have been discovered by surfers.

The golf courses of the southwest are a major attraction for visitors, the traditional links courses now joined by major new developments, such as the Robert Trent Jones-designed course at Adare Manor. Sea anglers are found along the region's long coastline, while game and coarse anglers are spoilt for choice on the region's lakes and rivers. Walkers have a range of looped and waymarked walks, cyclists can follow signposted trails, while surfers can make the most of the Atlantic swell on both south- and west-facing coasts.

For specific details on the activities mentioned below, check the Fáilte Ireland website: www.discoverireland.com.

GOLFING

The Irish are keen golfers, and it is seen as an accessible sport of the people, rather than a status symbol. The majority of clubs in the southwest are unstuffy places that welcome visitors, who are usually pleasantly surprised at the low price of green fees. The exceptions are the more expensive parkland courses such as Adare Manor, and the famous links courses, including Ballybunion, Tralee (built by Arnold Palmer), the Old Head of Kinsale and Waterville.

ANGLING

The Blackwater provides some of Ireland's finest fly-fishing, while boat operators offer day-long deep-sea

Gaelic Games

Hurling and Gaelic football arouse such passions that they are often described as a religion. These are fast-paced games, played by dedicated amateurs, organised around the parish and controlled by the Gaelic Athletic Association (GAA). Hurling is played with a wooden hurley, which can propel the ball along the ground, carry the ball aloft or throw it in the air. It is said to be one of the fastest ball games in the world, and is certainly one of the most exciting. Gaelic football, like hurling, is played by teams of 15-a-side, on the same size pitch with a round ball. It has similarities with rugby and association football, but throwing is not allowed. The main season runs from early summer, with regional finals in Cork's Pairc Ui Caoimh, culminating in the All-Ireland finals in Dublin's Croke Park in late September. For fixtures, see www.gaa.ie.

fishing trips from many coastal towns and villages, including Kinsale, Baltimore and Waterville. Pike and coarse angling are widely available in the Lee and Blackwater valleys.

WALKING

There is a wide choice of long-distance walking routes in the southwest, and a network of shorter looped walks of about one to three hours. It is easy to escape the crowds in such a sparsely populated region, and you can be walking in impressively wild, uninhabited terrain within an hour of landing at the airport.

CYCLING

Organised cycling holidays are increasingly popular, either travelling in a group with a back-up van, or cycling independently to pre-booked accommodation. The Ring of Kerry and Beara Way are signposted cycleways that hug the coastline for long stretches. Skibbereen has been designated a 'cycling hub', providing good accommodation and eating options, along with a choice of looped cycling routes to suit all levels of fitness.

ADVENTURE CENTRES

Learn sea-kayaking, canoeing, rock climbing, abseiling and other outdoor skills at a fast-growing network of outdoor adventure centres. Send the kids or book a family day out.

HORSE RIDING

There is a network of approved stables with qualified instructors. Choose between a residential riding holiday with tuition on a challenging cross-country course or ambles along country lanes on a hairy pony. Competent riders shouldn't miss the chance of trying an Irish sport horse on home ground.

SURFING

The southwest's beaches used to be empty in bad weather, with the exception of a few dog walkers. Now they are busy whatever the weather, with wet-suited surfers enjoying the large Atlantic rollers. Some surf schools offer tuition and equipment hire on the more benign beach breaks, while the more advanced can be towed out by jet-ski, hoping to catch one of the bigger waves.

Above from far left: fly-fishing on Glenbeg Lake; horseriders at Buttevant's Cahirmee Horse Fair.

Above: the Irish are big golfers; out hiking.

The Maharees
The Maharees is a 5km (3-mile) tombolo (sand spit) that divides Brandon Bay and Tralee Bay in County Kerry. Surfers delight in the Atlantic waves on the long sandy beaches, while the Maharees Islands attract sea anglers and divers. There's a 19km (12-mile) stretch of the Dingle Way walking trail parallel to the beach on Brandon Bay, where horseriding is also an option (O'Connor's Trekking; tel: 066-713 9216).

Left: surfing the Atlantic.

LITERARY HERITAGE

Ireland has a wonderfully strong literary heritage, and Cork and the southwest play their part in this, with writers from Elizabeth Bowen and William Trevor to Frank McCourt flying the flag for the region.

The first English-speaking writers associated with southwest Ireland were both young soldiers, sent there by Queen Elizabeth to help to pacify rebel Munster. Edmund Spenser (1552–99) wrote *The Faerie Queene*, the greatest poem of the period, while living at Kilcolman Castle in north Cork *(see tour 4)*. Sir Walter Raleigh visited him there in 1589. Elizabeth had given Raleigh a vast grant of land, including the walled town of Youghal *(see tour 2)*, which he sold in 1602.

MODERN WRITERS

Today north Cork is closely associated with two major novelists and short story writers, Elizabeth Bowen (1899–1973) and William Trevor (b.1928). Bowen's grave is at Farahy Church, beside the site of Bowen's Court (now demolished; *see tour 4*). The spirit of the last days of English rule, as described in her novel *The Last September*, from the viewpoint of the local 'big house' families, still lingers in this quiet rural corner.

Trevor was born in Mitchelstown, and spent his childhood in Youghal. Those familiar with his short stories will recognise the genesis of his ter-

ritory, in which genteel provincial souls live out lives of quiet desperation, in the less-frequented corners of today's southwest.

Among those involved in the struggle for Independence in the 1920s was Cork-born short story writer and critic, Frank O'Connor (1903–66). His story collection, *Guests of the Nation*, describes the era, as does Sean O'Faolain (1900–91), a fellow Cork-born Republican activist and writer. Both men, along with artist Robert Gibbings, frequented the Irish-speaking area around Inchigeelah and Gougane Barra *(see tour 3)*. They were lucky to experience the last days of a rural community that had changed little in the past 200 years.

The Anglo-Irish

Another society, that of west Cork's Anglo-Irish, whose ancestors were mainly soldiers in Oliver Cromwell's army, granted land in lieu of pay, is wittily described by Edith Somerville and Violet Martin, cousins who wrote as Somerville & Ross. Their best-known work, *Some Experiences of an Irish R.M.* (1899), pokes gentle fun at both the British magistrate

Films of the Southwest
To enhance your visual appreciation of the southwest, watch *Ryan's Daughter*, in which the scenery of the Dingle Peninsula far outshines the human stars, Robert Mitchum, Trevor Howard, Sarah Miles and John Mills; *Michael Collins* in which writer-director Neil Jordan takes an irreverent look at the hero of the Irish struggle for Independence; and *The Wind that Shakes the Barley*, a tense Civil War drama, filmed on location in west Cork by Ken Loach.

sent to impose order, and the ingenious, unruly characters he encounters. They are buried beside St Barrahane's Church in Castletownshend, 5km (3 miles) from Skibbereen *(see tour 5)*.

Island Writers

The Blasket Islands off the Dingle Peninsula *(see tour 10)* produced a number of writers at the turn of the 20th century, as linguists discovered an unusually pure Irish spoken there, and encouraged the writing of memoirs, including Peig Sayers' *Peig*, and Tomas O Crohán's *The Islandman*. The writers and their work are introduced in the Ionad (Heritage Centre) on the mainland, but it is worth reading *The Islandman* to get a vivid picture of island life. A wider history of this fascinating place is given in *The Blasket Islands – Next Parish America* (1980) by Joan and Ray Stagles.

On the Mainland

Listowel *(see tour 11)* was the home of publican John B. Keane (1928–2002), best known for his play *The Field*, filmed with Richard Harris. His work is set firmly in the rural community, and is by turn humorous and melodramatic. His memory is greatly revered in Listowel, and has led to an annual Writers' Week. A museum celebrates other locally born writers, including Maurice Walsh (1879–1964), whose short story was the inspiration for John Ford's film *The Quiet Man*.

Novelist Kate O'Brien (1897–1974), whose first novel, *Without My Cloak,* is an account of three generations of a Catholic family, used to be the sole famous writer from Limerick. But nowadays Frank McCourt (1930–2009), whose autobiography, *Angela's Ashes,* founded a new genre known as the 'misery memoir', is more famous.

Above from far left: Woulfe's Bookshop in Listowel; the town has a strong literary heritage: one of its famous sons is John B. Keane, commemorated in this statue.

Short-Story Prize
The Frank O'Connor Short Story Award offers a prize of €35,000 for the best collection of the year, the highlight of a short story festival held annually in September in Cork City *(see tour 1)*. www.munsterlit.ie.

Left: still from *Ryan's Daughter*, filmed on the Dingle Peninsula.

HISTORY: KEY DATES

Southwest Ireland has changed from being a traditional society of subsistence farmers and fishermen to a vibrant society that has embraced the best of 21st-century innovations without losing its unique identity.

EARLY PERIOD

6000BC	First traces of Stone Age people in southwest Ireland.
2000BC	First traces of Bronze Age people. The Celtic La Tène civilisation reaches Ireland.
AD1–500	Building of hill and ring forts.
500–800	Early Christian period.
9th century	Viking raids. Monasteries especially targeted for pillaging.
1014	Brian Boru defeats the Vikings.

ENGLISH CONQUEST

Stone Circles
Even though the megalithic remains of the southwest have now been fully documented, little is known about who built them and why. Drombeg Stone Circle *(see p.53)*, for example, was a Bronze Age ritual site, with carbon dating of 1127–795BC, and contained a burial urn with the bones of an adolescent. Anything beyond these facts is pure speculation.

1169	Norman invasion.
1537	Henry VIII orders the dissolution of the Irish monasteries.
1556	Elizabeth I of England 'plants' Munster with loyal Englishmen, including Walter Raleigh.
1601	Spanish and Irish forces defeated by English at Battle of Kinsale.
1649–52	Widespread destruction by Oliver Cromwell's army.
1689	James II lands in Kinsale with French support to reclaim throne.
1690	William of Orange's army reaches Kinsale following victory at Battle of the Boyne and attacks Charles Fort, which holds out for James.
1691	Irish Protestant parliament introduces the 'Penal Laws' denying Catholics the right to hold public office, own property or vote.

FREEDOM STRUGGLES

1796	Wolfe Tone's attempt to land French army in Bantry Bay is foiled.
1798	Crushing of United Irishmen's rebellion.
1800	Act of Union unites British and Irish parliaments at Westminster.
1829	Daniel O'Connell's Catholic Emancipation Bill carried.
1845–50	Failure of potato crop leads to the Great Famine; 1 million die and a further 2 million emigrate.

1849	Cove of Cork is named Queenstown after visit of Queen Victoria.
1875	Parnell becomes leader of the Home Rule Movement.
1885	Home Rule defeated in the House of Lords.
1912	The Irish National Volunteers formed to support Home Rule.

Above from far left: famine hit Ireland in the late 19th century, as depicted in *The Irish Famine, 1845–9* (artist unknown); *see feature box, p.54*; signing the 1921 treaty.

INDEPENDENCE AND AFTER

1916	Irish rebels are defeated in the Easter Rising.
1919	Guerrilla war between IRA and British irregulars, Black and Tans.
1921	Britain and Ireland sign a treaty granting Dominion status to most of Ireland, with six counties of Ulster remaining part of the UK.
1922–3	Civil war between pro- and anti-partitionists. Michael Collins is assassinated near Macroom.
1939–45	Ireland remains neutral in World War II.

A CHANGING WAY OF LIFE

1953	Last residents leave the Blasket Islands to live on the mainland.
1961	Television in the form of RTE1 reaches most of Cork and Kerry.
1969	'The Troubles' flare up again in Northern Ireland.
1973	Ireland joins European Community, now European Union (EU).
1991	Mary Robinson is elected President of Ireland.
1998–9	The historic Good Friday Agreement (1998) leads to an all-party assembly in Northern Ireland.
2002	The Republic adopts the euro.

BOOM TO BUST

2004	President Mary MacAleese returns for a second term of office. Smoking is banned in workplaces across Ireland, even pubs.
2005	Cork city is designated a European Capital of Culture. The IRA says its war is over, its weapons destroyed.
2007	Bertie Ahern wins third term as leader of a coalition government.
2008	After controversy over his finances, Ahern resigns. He is succeeded by his former deputy, Brian Cowen.
2009	Property crash during scandals over loans and bank regulation.
2010	Government takes measures to deal with unprecedented billions of 'toxic debt', including slashing public-sector pay and pensions.

Spanish Links
The ports of Dingle and Kinsale had strong maritime links with Cornwall, France and Spain, in contrast to Dublin which had links with England and Wales. If you sail due south from Kinsale, the first landfall you make will be on the north coast of Spain, east of La Coruña.

WALKS AND TOURS

1. Cork City   30

2. Cork Harbour and East Cork   36

3. Blarney Castle and
    the Lee Valley   42

4. Blackwater Valley and
    North Cork   46

5. Kinsale and Roaringwater Bay   50

6. Bantry Bay   56

7. The Ring of Beara   60

8. Killarney   64

9. The Ring of Kerry   68

10. The Dingle Peninsula   73

11. Tralee and North Kerry   77

12. Bunratty, Limerick and Adare   80

CORK CITY

After exploring Cork's indoor food market and renowned art gallery, climb to the neoclassical butter market and enjoy the views from Shandon's steeple. The vibrant university campus offers a combination of ancient and modern architecture. End the walk at a riverside park, home to the civic museum.

DISTANCE Full walk: 5km (3 miles); short walk 1.6km (1 mile)
TIME One to two days
START Grand Parade
END Fitzgerald Park
POINTS TO NOTE
Allow two days if you intend to visit all the attractions at the university. The walk can be shortened to one day, or 1.6km (1 mile), by finishing at the Cork Vision Centre. Note that Cork city is busiest on Saturday and quietest on Monday. Most city attractions are closed on Sunday or open only from 2pm. To avoid walking, take a no. 8 bus from St Patrick Street, or a short taxi ride to the university. Fota Island, the starting point of tour 2 *(see p.36)*, can be reached by train from Cork city, and is 17km (11 miles) to the east of the city on the N25.

Gallí Street Furniture
The striking modern street furniture of Grand Parade and St Patrick Street is a legacy of 2003, Cork's year as European Capital of Culture, and was designed by the Catalan architect, Beth Gallí. While it has created wider pavements, the jury is still out on the appropriateness of the huge lamp-posts.

Cork's city centre is built on an island formed by two channels of the River Lee. In the 18th and 19th centuries, cargoes of butter, beef and animal hides were exported from its many quays, creating a rich merchant class that built an attractive city of bridges and steeples, linked by wide streets lined with Georgian houses. The Shandon area, on a hill north of the Lee, was the location of the slaughterhouses and tanneries on which Cork's wealth was built, and the site of its butter market, which monitored the quality of this key export. The west of the city was developed later, its leafy residential areas expanding with the founding of University College in 1845, and the laying out of Fitzgerald Park in 1903.

CITY CENTRE

Start at the **Tourist Information Office** (tel: 021-425 5100; www.come tocork.ie) on **Grand Parade ❶**, a wide thoroughfare that is considered the city's central point. Directly across the road, note the terrace of three elegant Georgian houses with slate-hung, bow-fronted windows, remnants of Cork's 18th-century prime.

English Market
Turn right for the **English Market ❷** (Mon–Sat 9am–5pm), a Victorian

covered market. Step back to view the imposing classical entrance. A foodie-heaven, the market has about 150 stalls, from traditional butchers to purveyors of farmhouse cheeses and handmade chocolates; do not miss the alley of freshly landed seafood. Beside the entrance is the last purveyor in Cork of tripe and drisheen, a blood sausage made with sheep's and beef blood. In the poultry section look out for buttered eggs: buttering is believed to keep eggs fresh for up to six months.

Walking straight through the market will bring you to a piazza where **Farmgate Café**, see ⑪①, occupies an overhead balcony.

St Patrick Street

Turn left from the market into Princes' Street and then right onto **St Patrick Street** ③, a wide curved thoroughfare and the traditional place for a Saturday-afternoon promenade. Cross the street and follow Carey's Lane, a pedestrian alley, to **Paul Street** ④. It passes a small Huguenot graveyard. The area is now known as the Huguenot Quarter, and is Cork's 'left bank', with antiques shops, bookshops, art galleries, boutiques, cafés and buskers.

Crawford Municipal Art Gallery

At the northeastern end of Paul Street, the **Crawford Municipal Art Gallery** ⑤ (Emmet Place; tel: 021-490 7855; www.crawfordartgallery.ie; Mon–Sat 9am–5pm; free) is a large, Dutch-style red-brick building that dates from 1724; it was originally Cork's Custom House. The collection

Above from far left: English Market; the River Lee, which cuts through Cork city.

Above: Crawford Municipal Art Gallery.

Food and Drink 🍴

① FARMGATE CAFÉ
English Market, Princes Street; tel: 021-427 8134; Mon–Sat B, L and AT; €
A wonderful venue on a terrace above the bustling English Market. All the food they offer is sourced in the market; choose from home-made soups, quiches and imaginative open sandwiches or the more substantial table-service menu, which includes shepherd's pie and the catch of the day.

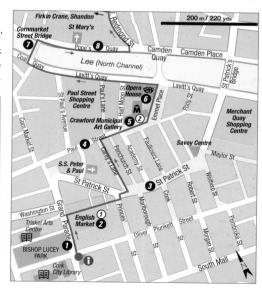

Above: exterior and plaque, Cork Opera House.

is strong on 18th- to 21st-century British and Irish painting and classical sculpture. Lovers of stained glass will enjoy the display of work by Harry Clarke (1889–1931), an Irish stained-glass artist of the Celtic Revival. The **Crawford Gallery Café**, see ⓘ②, is a favourite meeting spot that does excellent fresh food.

Cork Opera House

Turn left from the gallery and walk past the 1965 **Cork Opera House ❻** *(see p.20),* along a wide piazza. The huge award-winning glazed façade of the opera house dates from 2001. The piazza leads to the River Lee, with the steep northern side of Cork city opposite *(see margin, opposite).* Turn left (west) along Lavitt's Quay to the pedestrian **Cornmarket Street Bridge ❼.**

SHANDON

The Shandon district was the heart of working-class Cork before people were rehoused to the suburbs in the 1960s. Narrow lanes of cheek-by-jowl terraced houses, populated by a lively, local community, surround the butter market and St Anne's Church. In the 1980s the area was badly run-down, and was only rescued by the arrival of tourism and a new awareness of the importance of conserving local heritage.

Pope's Quay

Cross the pedestrian bridge to the long, handsome **Pope's Quay ❽**, named after the Widow Pope, the successful 18th-century business-woman who built it. **St Mary's Dominican Church**, with its impres-

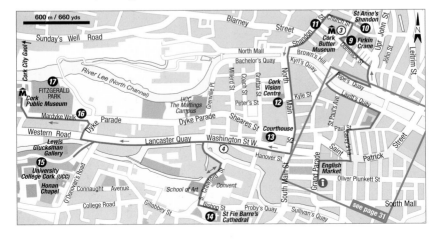

sive Ionic portico, dates from 1832, and is significant chiefly as the first large Catholic church to be erected in Cork after Catholic Emancipation was granted in 1829. Its considerable size was seen as a significant statement of the new confidence of the Catholic community.

The finely proportioned three-storey red-brick house beyond, **50 Pope's Quay**, is one of the few remaining samples of the architecture of early 18th-century Cork, and was saved from demolition thanks to voluntary fundraising. Red brick came in as ballast, and was considered superior to locally quarried stone.

Firkin Crane

Turn left up John Redmond Street, then take the first left to reach the **Firkin Crane** ❾. This neoclassical rotunda was the place where firkins (small barrels) of butter were once weighed and classified prior to export. (Today it is a performance space.)

The Firkin Crane was part of the **Butter Exchange**, to its north. Dating from 1796, it was once the largest butter market in the world. It now contains the **Shandon Craft Centre** (Mon–Sat 9am–5pm; free).

Next door is the **Cork Butter Museum** (O'Connell Square; tel: 021-430 0600; Mar–Oct daily 10am–5pm; charge), which tells the story of the Cork butter trade, and the folk culture behind it. **The Four Liars Bistro**, see

⑪③, next door to the museum, is a cheerful spot for a break.

St Anne's Shandon

The Four Liars takes its name from the four clocks on the four faces of the steeple of the neighbouring church, **St Anne's Shandon** ❿ (tel: 021-450 5906; Mon–Sat, Mar–Oct 9.30–4.30pm, Nov–Apr 10am–3.30pm; charge). This local nickname stems from the fact that its four clocks seldom all give the same time. The pepperpot steeple, the chief landmark of Cork's northside, was added to the church in 1749. The building is of red sandstone and white limestone, a popular combination of locally quarried stone. Because the sandstone is soft, limestone is used where cut stone is needed, usually in lintels and window surrounds. The effect is known as 'streaky bacon' after a favourite Cork food.

You can climb the 36m (120ft) steeple and play a tune on the church

Above from far left: the heart of Shandon; image of workers at the Firkin Crane, once part of a Butter Exchange and now a performance space; exterior of the Firkin Crane.

Sing-Song Accent
The northern side of the city rises steeply from the river, and wits like to joke that this is the origin of the distinctly 'up and down' Cork accent. You will hear fine examples of this on St Patrick Street in the afternoons, when newspaper sellers hawk the *Evening Echo* with loud cries of 'Eeeeeko'.

Food and Drink

② CRAWFORD GALLERY CAFÉ
Emmet Place; tel: 021-427 4415; same hours as gallery; €
This elegant room with tall windows is a restful haven. A team from Ballymaloe, Ireland's famous country house, offers light seasonal specials and legendary home-made cakes.

③ THE FOUR LIARS BISTRO
Butter Exchange, Shandon; tel: 021-439 4040; daily B, L and D; €–€€
This informal bistro brings a continental air to Shandon, with a quarry-tiled floor, wooden tables, muted background jazz and work by local artists on the walls. Steaks, pasta and local seafood are the owner-chef's specialities.

Prison Visit
Cork City Gaol and
Radio Museum
(Sunday's Well Road;
tel: 021-430 5022;
www.corkcitygaol.
com; daily Mar–Oct
9.30am–5pm, Nov–
Feb 10am–4pm;
charge) occupies an
imposing castle-like
building high above
the city on the
northwestern side.
The austere Victorian
gaol is inhabited by
life-size characters,
each with a sad story
to tell. The quaint
Radio Museum in the
Governor's House
displays genuine
artefacts that illustrate
the history of the early
days of Irish and
international radio
communication.

bells using card notations, or simply enjoy the splendid view of Cork City.

Shandon Street

Leaving St Anne's, go straight ahead down Church Street and left into **Shandon Street ⓫**. This area was the epicentre of Cork's cattle trade in the 18th century; such was the scale of the beef trade that Shandon was known as 'the slaughterhouse of Ireland'. Though cluttered by plastic signage, the street still has some good examples of 18th- and 19th-century Cork domestic architecture.

Cork Vision Centre

Cross the bridge at the foot of Shandon Street and continue straight on to enter what was once medieval Cork. The **Cork Vision Centre ⓬** (North Main Street; tel: 021-427 9925; free) is housed in the former Church of St Peter and Paul. The Centre hosts changing exhibitions on Cork's heritage and has a detailed 1:500-scale model of the city, showing how it has changed over the years.

WEST OF THE CITY CENTRE

Following the River Lee to the west of Cork city you quickly leave the realms of commerce and enter an area dominated by the university. Meanwhile, to the north, Victorian pleasure gardens line the riverbanks.

The Courthouse

Turn right out of the Cork Vision Centre and right on to Washington Street. You can't miss the **Courthouse ⓭**, an imposing building with a wide Corinthian portico, a pediment and a large copper dome. Built in 1835, it has recently been restored.

St Fin Barre's Cathedral

If you are walking to the university from the Courthouse, take a break at the riverside **Café de la Paix**, see ⑪④. On leaving, turn left on the bridge over the Lee and take the first right if you wish to visit **St Fin Barre's Cathedral ⓮**, Cork's Church of Ireland cathedral (Mon–Sat 9am–5.30pm, closed 12.45–2pm Oct–Mar; charge). If you don't want to go into the cathedral, continue west up Washington Street at this point instead.

Designed by William Burgess in 1870, St Fin Barre's is a compact building with a grand exterior in the French Gothic style. It has three spires and an elaborately carved west front, which is surmounted by a bronze angel. Contrastingly, its interior is relatively simple.

University College, Cork

From the cathedral, it is a pleasant 10-minute walk up Western Road (or hop on no. 8 bus) to the gates of **University College Cork ⓯** (Western Road; tel: 021-490 1876; www.ucc. ie; visitor centre: Mon–Fri 9am–

5pm; free), a constituent college of the University of Ireland, known as UCC, with almost 20,000 students. The 18-hectare (44-acre) campus is planted with mature shrubs and trees, including several giant redwoods. The **Visitor Centre** is in the north wing of the Tudor-Gothic-style quadrangle (1845). Beside it is a superb collection of Ogham stones inscribed with the Celtic alphabet. Other highlights include the Hiberno-Romanesque-style **Honan Chapel** (1916), on the upper part of the campus – a replica of Cormac's Chapel on the Rock of Cashel – neatly framed by eye-catching modern buildings. The chapel is a showcase for the Irish Arts and Crafts Movement, also known as the Celtic Revival. In contrast, the **Glucksman Gallery** (2005), on the lower part of the campus, won awards for its innovative architecture. It has exhibitions of contemporary art, and others complementing the activities of the College's art history department.

Mardyke Walk

Leave the campus by the main gates on to O'Donovan's Road, cross the Western Road and turn left on to the **Mardyke Walk** ⑯, a promenade lined with mature trees and popular with joggers and dog walkers. Adjoining is Cork's cricket ground; although a minority sport in Ireland, cricket is rapidly gaining a following after the country's success in the 2008 World Cup.

Fitzgerald Park

This leads to **Fitzgerald Park** ⑰, bordered on one side by the River Lee and on the other by the Mardyke, and laid out for the Cork Exhibition of 1903, with formal rose gardens and a pond. Within the park, **Cork Public Museum** (tel: 021-427 9925; Mon–Fri 11am–1pm, 2.15–5pm, Sat until 4pm, Apr–Sept also Sun 3–5pm; free) is set in a fine detached Georgian house with a new wing. Its collection focuses on the city's social, economic and political history, and includes an Iron Age La Tène period crown, 18th-century Cork silver and glass, and mementoes of Cork's role in Ireland's struggle for independence in the early 20th century.

Cork City Gaol *(see margin, left)* can be reached on foot by crossing the Daly Bridge from Fitzgerald Park to the north bank of the river. Alternatively, return to the Mardyke and stroll back into the city centre.

Above from far left: spires of St Fin Barre's Cathedral; religious carvings decorate the cathedral's pillars; gardens of University College.

Food and Drink 🍴

④ **CAFÉ DE LA PAIX BISTRO AND WINE BAR**
16 Washington Street; tel: 021-427 9556; daily B Mon–Fri from 8am, Sat from10am, Sun from noon, plus L and D; €–€€
This is a funky little place, with purple walls with lime trim and small glass tables. It backs on to the Lee and has tables outside. Its regular clientele enjoy the freshly prepared bistro-style menu and friendly service.

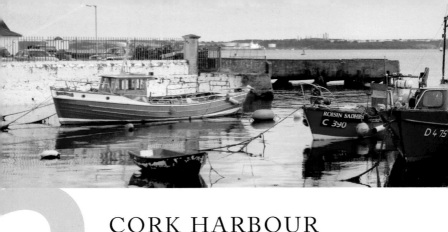

CORK HARBOUR AND EAST CORK

Visit Fota Island and Cobh, formerly Queenstown, the departure point for many Irish emigrants. Tour a 19th-century whiskey distillery, then discover Youghal's sandy beaches and its links with Walter Raleigh and Moby Dick.

DISTANCE 77km (48 miles)
TIME One or two days
START Fota Island
END Youghal
POINTS TO NOTE
Allow two days to visit all the attractions en route; one if you are cherry-picking. Trains run to Fota and Cobh half-hourly from Kent Station (Lower Glanmire Road; tel: 021-450 6766; www.irishrail.ie), on the city's northern side. The 25-minute train ride from Kent Station provides dramatic sea views that cannot be seen from a car. Return to Glounthaune Station for the branch line to Midleton, where a farmers' market takes place on Sat (10am–1pm). For an overnight stay consider Ballymaloe House in Shanagarry *(see p.40)*, or Bally-makeigh House *(see p.97)* near Youghal. From Youghal, you can continue to Cork on the N25 (48km/30 miles), or Blarney (58km/36 miles), turning off the N8 on to the N20 Limerick road.

Belvelly Smokehouse

About 1km (½ mile) beyond the gates of Fota House is Ireland's oldest traditional smoke-house. Frank Hederman supplies many fine restaurants and Fortnum and Mason with smoked salmon, silver eel, mackerel and mussels. Buy it vacuum packed from their shop, or eat it there (Belvelly, Cobh, Co. Cork; tel: 021-481 1089; www.frankhederman.com; Mon–Sat 9am–5pm).

Cobh, the port for the city of Cork, is 19km (12 miles) downstream from the city and faces south to the open sea beyond its lighthouse. The view of Cobh's steeply terraced houses beneath the soaring Gothic cathedral was the last, often tear-blurred, sight most emigrants had of their homeland.

East Cork, a low-lying area of arable farms with long sandy beaches, and a mild maritime climate, has a distinctive character that sets it apart from the more rugged character of the rest of southwest Ireland. Houses and cottage have tidy gardens with picket fences; some are even thatched, and at times it feels like being in England. This can perhaps be traced back to a combination of nautical liking for order (there are many seafarers settled in the area), and the long-term influence of the Quaker colony that is based in the Shanagarry area; one member, William Penn, left Cork in the late 17th century, and founded Pennsylvania. Midleton, a long-established market town with a large distillery, has always been a prosperous place. The coast between Ballycotton

and Youghal has many sandy beaches, and is largely undeveloped.

CORK HARBOUR

The north side of the harbour is formed by Fota Island and Great Island, linked to the mainland by causeways. Cobh, on Great Island, faces Cork's wide deep-water harbour and was the preferred first and last port of call for most transatlantic traffic during the 19th and early 20th centuries.

Fota Island

Leave Cork on the N8, taking the N25 Rosslare road at the Dunkettle Interchange. Turn off the N25 after 13km (8 miles) at the signpost for Fota and Cobh. **Fota Island ❶** is on the southern shore of Cork's outer harbour, linked to the mainland by a causeway. The 315-hectare (780-acre) estate, formerly owned by the family at Fota House, is surrounded by several kilometres of stone wall. Part of it now contains a golf course and luxury hotel.

Go to the second entrance for **Fota Wildlife Park** (tel: 021-481 2678; www.fotawildlife.ie; Mon–Sat 10am–4.30pm, Sun 11am–4.30pm; charge), which has giraffes, wallabies, ostriches, zebras and antelopes roaming free, plus a large outdoor enclosure for cheetahs. The car park (charge) also serves **Fota House, Gardens and Arboretum** (tel: 021-481 5543; www.fotahouse.com; gardens: daily 9am–6pm, free; house:

Apr–Oct Mon–Sat 10am–5pm, Sun 11am–5pm, last entry 4pm, Nov–Mar phone ahead; charge). The arboretum is over 200 years old and includes magnolias, rhododendrons and azaleas (at their best in late spring). The attractive Regency-style house was originally a shooting lodge; its servants' quarters retain many original features and are the main feature of the house tour. There are impressive plaster ceilings in the ground-floor reception rooms. A light menu of freshly prepared food is served in the house's south-facing, tall-windowed gallery, see ⑪①.

Cobh

The road from Fota to **Cobh ❷** (pronounced 'cove') skirts the edge of Cork Harbour for 6km (4 miles). On entering Cobh look out for a signpost to the right for Cobh Heritage Centre (free) and park beside it. The train station is next door.

The Centre occupies the old Victorian railway station beside the deep-water berth used by transatlantic liners. Cobh was the last port of call for the 'unsinkable' *Titanic* in 1912

Above: boats in Cork Harbour.

Above: Fota House.

Cork to Cobh Line
The railway from Cork to Cobh was designed by Isambard Kingdom Brunel. At times the train appears to float on water, making this undoubtedly one of the most beautiful commutes in the world.

Food and Drink

① **FOTA HOUSE CAFÉ**
Fota Island, Co. Cork; tel: 021-481 5543; daily, B, L, AT; €
The café occupies the Long Gallery, an elegant room, with well-spaced tables and views across the front lawn to farmland. The menu offers hot specials such as Ballycotton fish pie and shepherd's pie, plus home-made soups and quiches, salads and cakes.

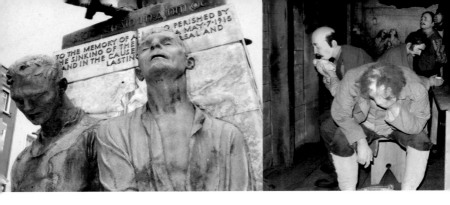

Farmers' Market

Midleton's Farmers' Market is popular for its locally grown potatoes, but also sells farmhouse cheeses, handmade chocolates and home-baked bread and cakes. It occupies the car park beside the first roundabout after the N25 from about 10am–1pm. The jazz trio that plays there puts everyone in a good mood.

and also received survivors and the drowned from the *Lusitania*, sunk off the coast by a German submarine in 1915. The Cove of Cork was renamed Queenstown after Queen Victoria's 1849 visit, and then Cobh (the Irish transliteration of Cove) in 1920.

Within the Centre, **The Queenstown Story** (tel: 021-481 3591; www.cobhheritage.com; daily 9.30am–5pm; charge) is a lively audiovisual display about the town's seafaring past and Irish emigration.

From the Centre, walk towards the town, an attractive south-facing Victorian resort, past the **Jacob's Ladder**, see ①②, a good food stop.

The Old Yacht Club (tel: 021-481 3301; offices: Mon–Sat 10am–5pm, gallery: Wed–Fri 11am–5pm, Sat–

Sun 2–5pm; free) is a waterside Palladian villa, built in 1854 for the Royal Cork Yacht Club, which was founded in 1720 and claims to be the oldest in the world. The club itself is no longer based here, and the beautiful villa, with balconies over the sea, is now shared by the Cobh Chamber of Tourism and the Sirius Arts Centre, a community exhibition and performance space.

The seafront has a Victorian town park, opposite which is the **Lusitania Memorial**, dedicated to the 1,198 people who died when the ocean liner sank on 7 May 1915. Along the seafront are the former offices of the Cunard Line and White Star Line. One of these was converted into a restaurant called The Titanic, which

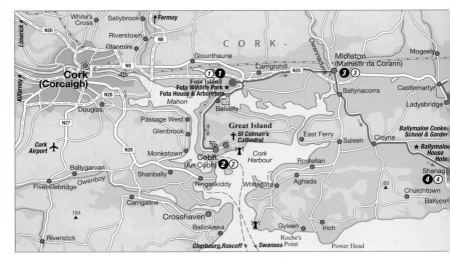

Above from far left:
Lusitania Memorial;
the Queenstown
Story; the neo-Gothic
St Colman's dom-
inates the seafront.

failed shortly after opening. Cobh was the last port of call for the ill-fated *Titanic* on 11 April 1912.

Overhead is the tall spire of the magnificent neo-Gothic **St Colman's Cathedral** (daily 9am–8pm; free), designed by E.W. Pugin (son of the more famous A.W.N. Pugin) and G. Ashlin. Building started in 1868, but its 90m (295ft) spire was not completed until 1919. The interior features a series of granite niches portraying the history of the Roman Catholic Church in Ireland. A free leaflet explains the interior in several languages. A 47-bell carillon rings out on the hour, and plays hymns at 9am, noon, 4pm and 6pm daily.

Walk up to the entrance of the cathedral for a fine view of Cork Harbour and its islands, with the open sea beyond. Note from here how the terraced houses are neatly stacked on this hillside; it is easy to see why one terrace is known locally as 'the pack of cards'.

To learn more about Cobh, join Michael Martin's **Titanic Trail**, a one-hour walking tour (meet outside Commodore Hotel, opposite the Old Yacht Club, at 11am daily; winter phone to confirm; tel: 021-481 3211; www.titanic-trail.com; charge).

EAST CORK

From Cobh return to the N25 and head east for about 8km (5 miles) to **Midleton ❸**, a pleasant market town with some attractive 18th-century

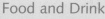

Food and Drink

② JACOB'S LADDER

Water's Edge Hotel, Cobh; tel: 021-481 5566; www.watersedgehotel.ie; daily B, L and D; €–€€
Jacob's Ladder is a clean-lined, contemporary bar-restaurant with a mesmerising panoramic harbour view. This is complemented by a varied and imaginative menu with an Irish accent: baked ham with parsley sauce, for example. It's also a great place to come for a coffee or a cocktail.

③ FARMGATE

The Coolbawn, Broderick Street, Midleton, Co. Cork; tel: 021-463 2771; Mon–Sat 9am–5pm, L, D Thur–Sat; €€–€€€
East Cork's favourite place for cake and gossip: enter through the shop, renowned for its cakes, bread, organic vegetables and artisan produce. The cooking is simple but effective; try crispy squid with chilli sauce, and don't miss the home-made desserts.

Quaker Influence
The Allen family of Ballymaloe are Quakers, and the area has a long association with the Society of Friends, or Quakers, who came from England in the late 17th century. Many settled here as farmers of fruit and vegetables, appreciating the mild climate and rich soil.

houses and a number of appealing artisan food shops.

Old Midleton Distillery
The **Old Midleton Distillery** (Distillery Walk, tel. 021-461 3594; www.jamesonwhiskey.com; daily 10am–6pm, last tour 4.30pm; charge) is at the far end of Midleton's main street from the town roundabout. Look out for Broderick Street halfway up on the right, location of the **Farmgate**, see 🍴③ *(p.39)*. The distillery tour explains the distilling process, and the site includes some impressive industrial architecture. The tour ends with a whiskey-tasting session.

Ballymaloe Philosophy
The better the ingredients you use, the better the food you'll cook. With this simple philosophy, Myrtle Allen began the Irish food revolution. Always a keen home cook, in 1964, with the children grown, she opened a restaurant in her dining room, serving fresh garden vegetables, fish from Ballycotton, local meat and home-made brown yeast bread. In an era when vegetables and fish were routinely boiled to death, and meat smothered in brown gravy, her light touch was a revelation. Her daughter-in-law, Darina, spread the word on television and in books, and in person at the Ballymaloe Cookery School at her farm on the other side of the village. Now a third generation, led by TV chef and author Rachel Allen, is carrying on the tradition. Recently, Darina has focused on forgotten skills, running courses on beekeeping, hen-keeping, home butchery and foraging, alongside demonstrations by top chefs from around the world.

Shanagarry and Ballymaloe
Return to the N25, and take the R629 for **Shanagarry** ❹. This is flat arable land, with carefully tended gardens. **Ballymaloe House**, see 🍴④, a famous country-house hotel on the approach to the village, is only open to guests, but you can drive in and visit the adjacent **Ballymaloe Cook's Shop**, which sells a selection of Irish crafts as well as cooks' paraphernalia.

Continue to the centre of the village about 1.6km (1 mile) on, and park at **Shanagarry Design Centre** (tel: 021-464 5838; daily 10am–6pm), a large craft outlet run by the Kilkenny Shop. The Centre sells crafts, including earthenware pottery by local Youghal potters, and by Stephen Pearce, another Shanagarry Quaker, whose distinctive bowls and tableware are much sought after by collectors. There is also a good selection of textiles, and a café. The gates across the road lead to **Shanagarry House**, the family home of Cork's most famous Quaker *(see margin, left)*, William Penn (1644–1718), the founder of Pennsylvania.

Return to the R629 (and an option to visit Ballycotton, *see margin, right*) and drive straight on for about 300m (1,000ft), turning left at the sign for **The Ballymaloe Cookery School and Gardens** (Kinoith, Shanagarry, Co. Cork; tel: 021-464-6785; www.cookingisfun.ie; gardens: daily 11am–5.30pm; charge), *see feature box, left*. The gardens feature free-ranging

hens, a potager, herb garden, Celtic maze, herbaceous borders and a shell house. There is also a farm shop here.

From here follow the R629 to **Garryvoe** ❺, a largely undeveloped seaside resort with a big sandy beach with views of the lighthouse at Ballycotton. It's a great place for a beach walk at any time of year. Rejoin the N25 eastbound at Castlemartyr. From here it is 18km (11 miles) to Youghal.

Youghal

Youghal ❻ is a seaside town with 5km (3 miles) of sandy beaches on its southern approach. To reach the main street, drive on through the **Clock Tower**, a distinctive landmark built in 1776 as a gaol and also used as a hangman's gibbet. The steps beside it lead to a street of handsome Georgian houses with excellent views of the wide harbour (the estuary of the mighty River Blackwater), and the 13th-century **St Mary's Collegiate Church**. The house next door, **Myrtle Grove**, was home to Sir Walter Raleigh until 1602. Raleigh is said to have smoked the first tobacco and planted the first potato plant in Ireland there (a claim made by several other places).

At this point, return to ground level by walking downhill from the church, and cross the main street towards the town's quays. In 1956, during the production of *Moby Dick*, the North American director John Huston filmed the New Bedford scenes here. In spite of some incongruous Celtic Tiger apartment blocks, the place is still recognisable, as you will see from the photographs in Paddy Linehan's pub, with its gable-end Moby Dick mural.

A few steps further south along the quays is **Youghal Heritage Centre** (Market Square; tel: 024-20170; 9am–5pm, June–Aug daily, Sept–May Mon–Fri; free). Guided walking tours leave here at 11am daily. A short walk to the north and back on to Main Street will lead you to Youghal's famous seafood bar, **Aherne's**, see ⑪⑤.

Above from far left: whiskey-making equipment (*left and centre*) at the Old Midleton Distillery; Paddy Linehan's pub in Youghal.

Ballycotton

If you like fishing villages with brightly painted trawlers, clifftop walks and soaring seabirds, then Ballycotton, 5km (3 miles) south from Shanagarry, is worth a detour. Famous locally for its lifeboat, it has an RNLI shop, selling lifeboat-themed items and with great views of its lighthouse, scenically located on a tiny offshore island.

Food and Drink 🍴

④ BALLYMALOE HOUSE
Shanagarry, Co. Cork; tel: 021-465 2531; daily L, D; €€€–€€€€
A meal at the source of the Irish food revival will be one to remember. Fresh local produce, much of it from their farm, is cooked in an unfussy contemporary style and served in gracious traditional surroundings. Book in advance. Open to guests only.

⑤ AHERNE'S SEAFOOD BAR AND RESTAURANT
163 North Main Street, Youghal, Co. Cork; tel: 024-92424; daily, bar L, D €, restaurant, D €€€–€€€€
The traditional bar serves simple seafood (prawns in garlic butter, seafood pie topped with mashed potatoes, oysters fresh from the local trawlers, etc), while the formal restaurant offers a more ambitious menu, including hot, buttered lobster.

BLARNEY CASTLE AND THE LEE VALLEY

This tour visits Ireland's most famous castle, set in beautiful parklands and the showpiece of an attractive village. Afterwards, leave the crowds behind and follow the River Lee to its source, the mountain lake, Gougane Barra.

DISTANCE 87km (53 miles)
TIME One day
START Blarney
END Ballylickey
POINTS TO NOTE

There are frequent buses from Cork city to Blarney, leaving Parnell Place Bus Station (tel: 021-450 8188; www.buseireann.ie). A car is essential for the drive part of this tour. The drive takes about an hour and a half direct, or a leisurely half-day. At Ballylickey turn left on the N71 for Bantry (5km/3 miles) and Durrus (16km/10 miles), the latter being the starting point of tour 6, Bantry Bay. Or turn right for Glengarriff 12km (8 miles), Adrigole 30km (19 miles) further on being the starting point of tour 7, Ring of Beara. Alternatively, return to Cork direct on the N71 (90km/56 miles) – a pleasant 1.5-hour drive.

Castle Restoration

Thirty years ago many of the castles in the southwest were in a similar state of disrepair to Carrigadrohid, but there has been a surge in castle restoration in Ireland lately. The most famous enthusiast is probably the actor Jeremy Irons, who restored the ruin of Kilcoe Castle near Skibbereen, transforming it into a comfortable home, while retaining its original features. He has described castle restoration as 'a very expensive hobby'.

With not one but three castles en route – even if one is usually submerged – this is a distinctly romantic meander through some lush and increasingly spectacular countryside.

BLARNEY

Blarney ❶ 10km (6 miles) northwest of Cork city is now surrounded by suburbs. However, the village, which is bypassed, has retained its distinctive character, with small houses built around a central green in the shadow of the huge castle.

Blarney Castle

After leaving the N22 for Blarney, turn left beyond the second patrol station for the village. On the far side of the green is **Blarney Castle** (tel: 021-438 5252; www.blarneycastle.ie; daily 9am–sundown, Sun until 5.30pm in summer; charge), a massive 16th-century fortified home, consisting of a tall tower adjoining a shorter but stouter battlemented keep. The castle is situated in 160 hectares (400 acres) of landscaped park with rock gardens and a large lake. The building, rising up from a huge limestone base, reaches a height of 26m (85ft), with walls that

in places are 6m (18ft) thick. Like most castles, it is built on high ground near a source of fresh water, in a strategically important position. Although the castle is not furnished, all the rooms are intact – from the chapel and banqueting hall to the dungeon.

To reach the top, from where there are commanding views you have to climb a spiral staircase with 84 stone steps. There is a one-way system, up one spiral staircase and down another.

Blarney Stone

The word 'blarney' has come to mean flattering cajoling talk and is believed to have its origin in the excuses made to England's Queen Elizabeth I by the then Lord Blarney, reluctant to surrender his castle to the Crown.

The link between the stone and acquiring 'the gift of the gab' has never been explained, but was a tradition by 1800. To kiss the **Blarney Stone**, you need to lie on your back and lean your head out over the castle's ramparts while being held securely by staff who handle some 300,000 stone-kissers a year.

Escape the tour bus crowds at the **Blarney Castle Hotel**, see ⑨①, by turning left as you leave the compound, not following the herd straight on.

LEE VALLEY

The lower reaches of the River Lee (which reaches the sea at Cork city) have been dammed to create hydro-

electricity. Further west the river runs through a rare alluvial forest, before turning into a scenic lough, then a stream and arriving at its source.

Inniscarra Dam

Leave Blarney on the R617 west through Tower, turning right after about 3km (2 miles) on to the R579 (signposted Kanturk), then almost immediately bearing left on to the R622 and turning right on to the R618. The road follows the north bank of the Lee, which is on your left. Shortly after the first glimpse of the 224m (800ft) dam and the hydroelectric station at **Innishcarra ❷**, there is viewing point for **Innishcarra Lake**. The river valley was flooded in 1957, a controversial project resisted by families who had farmed there for generations. When the water is low, you can sometimes see the towers of a submerged castle.

Carrigadrohid Castle

Beyond the dam is an attractive rural drive of around 14km (8.5 miles) to **Carrigadrohid ❸**, a tiny crossroads village. Stop and park and walk to the left to the wall of the dramati-

Above from far left: Blarney House, a 19th-century mansion in the castle grounds; Blarney Castle.

Above: Blarney Castle's tower and keep; there is no dignified way of kissing the Blarney Stone.

Food and Drink

① BLARNEY CASTLE HOTEL
The Square, Blarney; tel: 021-438 5116; www.blarneycastlehotel.com; B, L, D; €
Dating from 1837, this traditional inn overlooks the village green. Eat local seasonal produce in the pub or the Lemon Tree Restaurant. Famous scones.

Robert Gibbings
One of the first to praise the River Lee was the Cork-born artist and writer, Robert Gibbings (1889–1958). He lived in England, where he ran the Golden Cockerel Press. He found commercial success during World War I with a series of illustrated books describing leisurely expeditions on the Thames, the Wye and the Seine, and *Lovely is the Lee*, which is still in print in Cork. He is still remembered fondly in Inchigeelagh and Gougane Barra.

cally sited **Carrigadrohid Castle** (no access), built by the MacCarthy clan (who also built Blarney) around 1455. It is on a rocky island in a narrow stretch of the Lee, connected to either side by an ancient stone bridge. The four walls are standing, but there are wide cracks in the gable end. There is an unpaved riverside woodland path on the far side of the bridge, where the birdsong is amazing.

There is a second power station upriver from Carrigadrohid, and the lake it created can be seen intermittently on your left as you continue to Macroom (8km/ 5 miles). Turn east (towards Cork city) on the N22 for about 1km (½ mile), then right on to the R584.

The Gearagh

After about 5km (3 miles) you will notice an extraordinary, seemingly derelict, landscape on your left. This is **The Gearagh ❹,** a glacial area of alluvial forest with oak, ash and birch growing on a maze of little islands. Just beside the car park is a causeway, from which you can observe the area's wildlife and its rich diversity of plants, insects and mammals, including stoats and otters.

Inchigeelagh

The land becomes rockier approaching **Inchigeelagh ❺**, a small village in the Muskerry Gaeltacht (Irish-speaking area), under the shadow of the Shehy Mountains (548m/1,800ft). This is the home territory of the O'Leary clan. Here, the Lee becomes Lough Allua, a narrow, reed-fringed lake, dotted with wild water lilies, equally beloved of artists and anglers. The village is a place that time forgot: rent a wooden rowing boat beside the lake, for a few hours of unforgettable peace. Joe Creedon, artist, and owner of **Creedon's Hotel**, see ⑪②, is a fount of local knowledge.

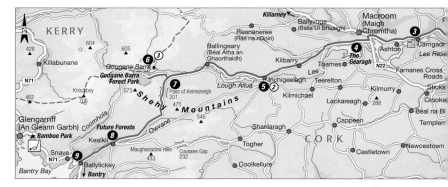

Gougane Barra

Drive on for 15km (9 miles) through **Ballingeary** (see ⑪③) and some of the best lake and mountain scenery in the southwest, to **Gougane Barra** ❻. The source of the River Lee is one of Ireland's most famous beauty spots: a tarn of black water, under looming mountain cliffs. It is said St Finbar killed a monster here before setting up a hermitage in the 6th century. Nothing remains of this; the tiny Romanesque-style oratory dates from the 20th century, while the ruins around it date from the 18th century. Gougane Barra Forest Park consists of 400 hectares (1,000 acres) of woodland, with a choice of paths. Note the award-winning thatched toilets.

PASS OF KEIMANEIGH

Return to the R584 and head south through a glacially formed mountain pass. The dramatic **Pass of Keimaneigh** ❼ (the pass of the deer) is a

steep-sided cutting through the Shehy Mountains, formed by erosion as the ice-age glaciers melted.

These remote parts of west Cork have attracted many settlers, often of a New Age mind-set. One of the most successful ventures is **Future Forests** ❽ (Kealkil, Co. Cork; tel: 027-66176), a garden centre cleverly built from rough timber that has revived traditional local skills, including hedging, thatching and dry-stone walling. Future Forests works closely with garden designer Mary Reynolds, whose career took off when her Celtic Garden won a Gold Medal at the Chelsea Flower Show in 2002.

The road reaches the coast at **Ballickey** ❾, a sheltered wooded inlet on Bantry Bay, famous for its mussels.

Turn left for Bantry and Cork city, or right for Glengarriff.

Above from far left:
The Gearagh *(far left; centre)*; Gougane Barra woods.

St Finbar's Day
The first Sunday after St Finbar's feast day (29 September) still attracts thousands of pilgrims to Gougane Barra. A pipe band processes to Finbar's oratory, where an open-air mass is celebrated. Some pilgrims walk over the mountain from Kilgarvan in Co. Kerry, a distance of about 19km (12 miles), as they have done for generations. Finbar, also spelt Finbarr, remains a popular Cork name *(see p.34)*.

Food and Drink 🍴
② **CREEDON'S HOTEL**
Carraig Liath, Inchigeelagh; tel: 026-49012; http//inchigeelagh.net; May–Sept, bar daily, L Sat–Sun; €
This is a quiet, old-fashioned village hostelry remarkable chiefly for its friendly hosts Joe and Ann Creedon. The food is hearty and traditional, served beside an open fire amid modest antiques and Robert Gibbings' watercolours.

③ **GOUGANE BARRA HOTEL**
Ballingeary, Co. Cork; tel: 026-47069; www.gouganebarra hotel.com; B, L daily, D Mon–Sat; €€–€€€
One of Ireland's most romantic hotels, this family-run establishment commands a prime view of lake and mountain. The restaurant is popular for Sunday lunch (booking advisable), while a freshly prepared menu including seafood and home baking is served in the bar and lounge.

4

BLACKWATER VALLEY AND NORTH CORK

After walking around Lismore, one of Ireland's most beautiful villages, the drive follows the Blackwater River inland through fertile farmlands, and impressive stands of mature trees. Attractions en route include the romantic Annes Grove Garden, a 2000BC wedge tomb, and peaceful monastic ruins.

DISTANCE 109km (68 miles)
TIME Walk, about an hour, then a full day's drive.
START Lismore
END Mallow
POINTS TO NOTE
Lismore is 31km (19 miles) north-west of Youghal, the end of tour 2. Mallow is 66km (41 miles) east of Killarney, starting point of tour 8; the N72 is an alternative scenic route to Killarney, with lighter traffic. Kinsale, the starting point of tour 5, is 71km (44 miles) south of Mallow.

Lismore Castle

This castle was owned by Sir Walter Raleigh, who sold it in 1602 to the Earl of Cork. It passed by marriage to the Devonshire family in 1753. The village was built to house the workers on the Duke of Devonshire's estates. The Duke, as he is known locally, whose English home is Chatsworth in Derbyshire, owns 34km (21 miles) of prime fishing on the Blackwater. A 1.6km (1-mile) stretch of river is currently worth around €500,000. Youghal County Council are using 17th-century documents to challenge the Duke's title to certain stretches of the river.

The Blackwater is the second-largest river in Ireland, famous for salmon fishing. It rises in the mountains on the Cork-Kerry border, and flows east to Lismore, reaching the sea at Youghal *(see p.41)*. The Blackwater Valley was woodland until the 17th century, and many fine trees still flourish.

North from the Blackwater are the rich plains of north Cork. Among those who settled in its idyllic country-side were monks brought to Ireland by the Anglo-Norman settlers. The area has a rich literary heritage and some notable Georgian architecture.

LISMORE

Arriving at **Lismore** ❶ from the south on the N72, as you cross the Black-water River there is a dramatic view of **Lismore Castle** (closed to the public), perched on an escarpment above the river. This mid-19th-century building is the Irish residence of the Duke of Devonshire *(see margin, left)*.

Park in the centre and walk to the **Lismore Heritage Centre** (tel: 058-54975; www.discoverlismore.com; Mon–Fri 9am–5.30pm, May–Oct also Sat 10am–5.30pm and Sun noon–5.30pm; charge), formerly the town courthouse.

Village Walk

Turn right and walk along Lismore's main street. Among the pleasant mix of shops and antiques stores are several pubs, including **O'Brien Chophouse,**

Above from far left: fountain in Lismore; Lismore Castle; hiker at Labbacallee, site of three huge capstones.

see ⑪①. Turn left up the broad North Mall, which leads to **St Carthage's Cathedral** (daily 9.30am–5.30pm; free), a modest mid-17th-century church in the neo-Gothic style. Take the cobbled footpath to the left of the church leading downhill, and turn left at the main road back to the car park.

Just here is the entrance to **Lismore Castle Gardens and Art Gallery** (tel: 058-54424; www.lismorecastle.com; daily Apr, May and Sept 1.45–4.45pm, June–Aug 11am–4.45pm; charge). The 3 hectares (7 acres) of gardens consist of woodland walks and contemporary sculpture, with good castle views.

FERMOY

Leave Lismore on the N72 heading east (in the direction of Waterford), and immediately after crossing the bridge over the Blackwater, turn left on to the R666 to Fermoy (27km/16.5 miles), a bucolic riverside route, offering good views of the Blackwater. The R666 reaches the north of **Fermoy** ❷, near the town park. Park and walk across the bridge, turning right on a riverside path to view the weir. A pedestrian alley from the riverwalk leads to the main road, and **Munchies Eating House**, see ⑪②.

Fermoy was established in the late 18th century, and most of its buildings date from the 19th century, when it was an important crossroads on the Cork–Dublin and Waterford–Mallow roads. The large *porte-cochère* of the Grand Hotel beside the bridge is a legacy of Fermoy's importance as a coaching stop in the 19th century. British army barracks were built north of the river, while schools and Catholic churches dominate the south side.

LABBACALLEE

Head west on the N72, looking left for a view of Fermoy's south bank topped by a line of Victorian schools and churches. Turn almost immediately right on to the R512. A brown signpost at the first fork leads to **Labbacallee Megalithic Wedge Tomb** ❸ about 1km (½ mile) on. Built over 4,000 years ago, it is one of the biggest in Ireland, with three large capstones. Climb the stile for a closer look. Excavations in 1934 revealed a number of ancient burials

Food and Drink

① O'BRIEN CHOP HOUSE
Main Street, Lismore, Co. Waterford; tel: 058-53810; Wed–Sat L 12.30–2.30pm, D 6–10pm, Sun 12.30–8pm; €–€€
Victorian pub with a traditional dark interior leading to a pretty garden. It is known for robust versions of traditional Irish food – steak and kidney pie with spring greens, fish pie with garden salad – sourced locally and served simply.

② MUNCHIES EATING HOUSE
Lower Patrick Street, Fermoy; tel: 025-33653; Mon–Sat until 5pm, B, L, AT; €
Tables on raised decking outside give a continental air to this busy, friendly café. It serves excellent coffee, and everything is freshly prepared on the premises: try bangers (sausages) and mash, followed by bread-and-butter pudding.

in the chamber, including one of a woman: its Irish name means 'bed of the old hag'. At the equinoxes, the setting sun illuminates the inner chamber through a small square hole. This is the biggest of various megalithic remains in the area.

AROUND CASTLE HYDE

Retrace your steps to the N72, and drive west. The large gates on the left after about 3km (2 miles) belong to **Castle Hyde**, an imposing late Georgian house overlooking the Blackwater. It was the ancestral home of Ireland's first President, Douglas Hyde (1860–1949). Today it belongs to *Riverdance* star, Michael Flatley, who has extensively renovated it. A fine stand of ancient beech trees lines the extensive boundary wall.

This is stud farm country, and on the opposite side of the N72 many million-euros worth of Irish bloodstock graze the lush pastures.

At **Ballyhooly** ❹, a small village beloved of anglers, a bend of the N72 passes H.M. Grindel, a tiny old-fashioned pub patronised by football legend (and former Ireland manager) Jack Charlton, as well as numerous anglers.

Bridgetown Priory

Follow the brown signpost to the left about 1.6km (1 mile) beyond Ballyhooly, and take the first left. From the hill you can view the extensive ruins of the 13th-century **Bridgetown Priory** ❺ (freely accessible) in a sheltered hollow beside the Blackwater, a wonderfully peaceful spot. The river is hidden by tall trees in summer.

NORTH CORK

The tour continues into North Cork. The River Awbeg flows into the Black-

Above: Bridgetown Priory ruin and Celtic cross carving.

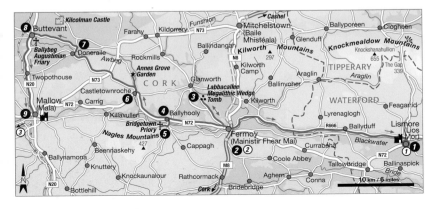

water at **Castletownroche** ❻. Park to view the mill race and the contrasting still water. The Roches were the Anglo-Norman overlords hereabouts, and the name is still common. Continue up the hill, taking the right fork for Doneraile. After 1.5km (1 mile) the road forks again. Go right to visit **Annes Grove Garden** (tel: 022-26145; mid-Mar–Sept Mon–Sat 10am–5pm, Sun 1–6pm; charge), the highly romantic garden of a compact Georgian house, planted in the informal Robinsonian style, incorporating riverside walks.

Doneraile

Return to the fork and double back for **Doneraile** ❼. Turn right on arriving at the village, down a wide street lined with Georgian houses. **Doneraile Park** (tel: 087-251 5965; daily, Apr–Oct 8am–8pm, Nov–Mar 8am–5pm; free) is on the right. This is a superb 18th-century park, landscaped in the 'Capability Brown' style, with a lake, mature trees and a herd of red deer. The Doneraile area has many literary associations *(see margin, right)*.

Buttevant

Turn right from the park and left at the first crossroads for **Buttevant** ❽, a small village with a wide main street. The street is still the venue for the annual Cahirmee Horse Fair, on 12 July. The first ever steeplechase (6.5km/4 miles) was run in 1752 from Buttevant to Doneraile.

At Buttevant turn left on the N20. The Catholic parish church on the left has the charming ruins of a 13th-century Franciscan abbey in its grounds. Continue for 2km (1 mile) for **Ballybeg Augustinian Friary**, 13th-century monastic ruins with a well-preserved dovecote.

Mallow

Continue south to **Mallow** ❾, once a prosperous spa and market town on the Blackwater River. To visit a superb Irish 'big house', take the N72 west at the second roundabout for 5km (3 miles) to **Longueville House**, see ⑪③. Otherwise follow the signpost to the town centre, which has a clockwise one-way system. At the bottom of the hill, just beyond the petrol station, keep an eye out to the left for the entrance to **Mallow Castle** (free). The tall ruins of an Elizabethan mansion are in a public park with a herd of white fallow deer, descended from a pair donated by Queen Elizabeth over 400 years ago.

Above from far left: wild flowers, house and mill stones at Castletownroche.

Literary Heritage
Bookworms should follow the brown signposts in the area for the literary heritage trail. To the east (from Doneraile) at Farahy, near Kildorrery, the grave of Elizabeth Bowen (1899–1973, *see p.24*) is in a small country churchyard. To the north are the remains of Kilcolman Castle, where Edmund Spenser (1552–99) wrote his epic poem, *The Faerie Queene*.

Food and Drink

③ LONGUEVILLE HOUSE

Mallow, Co. Cork; tel: 022-47156; www.longuevillehouse.ie; L Wed–Sat, bar food 1–5pm, Sun restaurant, D Wed–Sun; €€–€€€€

Longueville House is a large 1720 Palladian-style mansion in 200 hectares (500 acres) of parkland on the Blackwater. The O'Callaghan family offers low-key luxury, well worth the premium for bar food, while the haute cuisine in the conservatory at dinner will be memorable.

KINSALE AND ROARINGWATER BAY

Spend a day exploring the coastline of rural west Cork, starting in Kinsale, a historic port turned fashionable resort, then meandering along the rocky coast of Roaringwater Bay, through colourful fishing villages packed with enticing hostelries.

DISTANCE 95km (51 miles)
TIME One day
START Kinsale
END Schull
POINTS TO NOTE
A car is essential for this tour. At the end, either return to Kinsale on the N71 via Innishannon (97km/60 miles), or stay in the Schull-Skibbereen area. Durrus, the start of tour 6 *(see p.56)*, is 24km (15 miles) north of Schull.

Seven Heads Walk
Timoleague is the start of the Seven Heads Walk, a 42.5km (26½-mile) route. The initial (3.2km/2-mile) stretch follows the route of the West Cork Railway along the water's edge from Timoleague to Courtmacsherry, and is totally flat. The path runs around a headland known as Seven Heads offering great seaviews, bluebell woods, meadows of wild flowers, sandy beaches and a good chance of spotting seals and porpoises. www.sevenheads peninsula.ie.

Once a run-down rural backwater, the west Cork coast is so close to Cork Airport and Cork City and is known for having such friendly locals and an unspoilt environment that many people have bought holiday homes in the area; others have relocated permanently, bringing prosperity and a cosmopolitan air to the region. This drive heads west to explore the villages around the coast of Roaringwater Bay, and includes the option of visiting a couple of islands.

KINSALE

Kinsale **❶**, a small town 29km (18 miles) south of Cork city, overlooks the estuary of the Bandon River. Its sheltered harbour has always been a busy fishing port. Following the departure of a large British army garrison in 1921, it went into a decline, which was only reversed in the late 1970s with its development as a resort known for its restaurants, yachting and, most recently, the Old Head of Kinsale Golf Links.

Charles Fort
Approaching Kinsale from Cork, look out for a signpost to **Charles Fort ❹** (tel: 021-477 2263; www. heritageireland.ie; daily mid-Mar–Oct 10am–6pm, Nov–mid-Mar until 5pm; charge), 2km (1 mile) outside town, on the outer harbour. This massive star-shaped fort encloses 3 hectares (8 acres) of land and was built in 1680 as a harbour defence. In clear weather you can see the **Old Head of Kinsale**, the western extremity of the fjord-like harbour.

A footpath runs along the shoreline from the east of the fort to the outer harbour for about 2km (1 mile), offering excellent sea views. You can also walk out to Charles Fort from Kinsale, taking a footpath along the water's edge towards the village of Summercove. If you're coming by car, drive north along the coast road into town.

Town Walk

The narrow streets and tall Georgian houses of Kinsale are clustered around the sides of a conical hill. Before becoming a fashionable resort, Kinsale was best known for the Battle of Kinsale (1601), in which the combined forces of the (Catholic) Irish army, and a force of 3,814 Spanish infantry led by Don Juan del Aguila, were defeated by the (Protestant) English. After this rout the Irish clan chiefs left for Europe and never returned. Kinsale retained trading links with Spain and Holland both of which left a mark on its architecture, and give the town a continental air unusual in rural Ireland.

Park on the quay below the **Spaniard Pub**, walk straight on up Pearse Street and turn left for the **Court House B**. The symmetrical slate-hung building dates from 1706, and has a ground-floor arcade, and three Dutch gables. Upstairs is the **Kinsale Museum** (Market Square; tel: 021-477 7930; Mon–Sat 11am–5pm, Sun 3–5pm; free). It contains a miscellany of curiosities ranging from the boots

of the Kinsale giant to mementos of the sinking of the *Lusitania* off the Old Head of Kinsale in 1915.

From the back of the Court House, walk towards the salmon-shaped weather vane on the tower of **St Multose C**. The church dates from *c.*1200, and the nave retains its 13th-century layout. It has a stone-walled graveyard, where some of the victims of the sinking of the *Lusitania* are buried.

Turn right leaving St Multose and take the first left for **Desmond Castle D**, a 15th-century tower house, containing the **International Museum of Wine** (Cork Street; tel: 021-477 4855; www.winegeese.ie; mid-Apr–Oct daily 10am–6pm; charge). The displays cele-

Above from far left: Kinsale town and harbour; bilingual road signs.

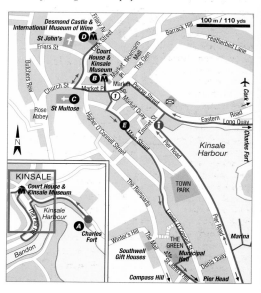

brate the Irish families who took up wine-making after leaving for France in the 17th century; their names include Hennessy, Barton, Lynch and Dillon.

Check out Kinsale's reputation for high-quality food by visiting **Cucina**, see ⑪①. Turn right out of Cucina and walk down Kinsale's **Main Street ⑤**, a narrow backstreet, main street of the medieval walled town. It now contains a lively collection of shops, galleries and restaurants. At the junction with Emmett Street you will see the **Tourist Information Office** (Pier Road; tel: 021-477 2234; www.kinsale.ie).

Continue to Lower O'Connell Street, and walk up **Green Lane** – the steps on your right leading to the **Municipal Hall**, a stone building with tall Gothic windows overlooking the harbour, fronted by a bowling green. Continue to the **Mall** for a panoramic view of the harbour. Behind are the **Southwell Gift Houses**, built in 1682, and still inhabited. A signpost

leads to **Compass Hill**, a circular walk which takes about 45 minutes. To return to the town centre go down **St John's Hill**, past some attractive Georgian houses, to the **Pier Head**, where visiting trawlers tie up. From here you can walk along **Pier Road**, past the yacht marina, to your car.

THE ROAD TO SKIBBEREEN

The R600 crosses the River Bandon heading west to quieter country where a slower pace of life prevails.

Timoleague

It winds along the shores of an estuary for 9km (5½ miles), with views of Courtmacsherry, a colourful fishing village on the far shore. At low tide the mudflats are home to a variety of shore birds, and large flocks of migrants winter here. At the start of the scenic section of the R600, just

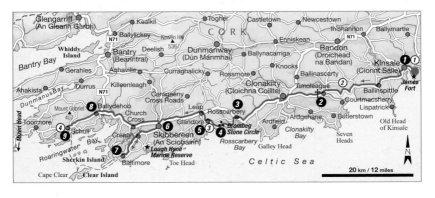

beyond a huge, usually empty sandy beach, look out for **The Pink Elephant**, see ⑪②, a beautifully located bar. As you approach **Timoleague ❷**, a sleepy village with tranquil sea views, you can see the ruins of **Timoleague Abbey** (free) at the top of the inlet. It is a 14th-century Franciscan friary, whose layout can be traced in the ruins. Photographers will enjoy picturing the estuary through its tall lancet windows.

Rosscarbery

You will only glimpse **Clonakilty**, a pretty market town with traditional wooden shop fronts and carefully tended floral displays, as you bypass it on the N71. **Rosscarbery ❸** is approached by a causeway across a sea inlet, where large flocks of swans glide by. Rosscarbery was an important monastic centre in the 6th century, famous for its school. The village square is on a hill above the main road. Rosscarbery Cathedral, to the north of the square, is a small 13th-century church, largely rebuilt in the 19th century.

Drombeg Stone Circle

About 200m/yds outside the village, take the R597 west (left) for Glandore. After about 5km (3 miles) a sign leads to the **Drombeg Stone Circle ❹**, sited on a plateau facing the distant sea. This is one of the most complete of the region's early Bronze

Age remains. A burial, carbon-dated to 1124–794BC, was excavated at the centre of the ring of 14 stones, but nobody knows who built the circle nor what it signified to them. Locally, it is believed to be in alignment with the setting sun at the winter solstice. Beside it is a Bronze Age cooking pit, with a full explanation.

Millionaire's Row

Continue west to **Glandore ❺**, a line of south-facing houses perched

Above from far left: walking the dog on Courtmacsherry Bay, between Timoleague and Kinsale; remote spot by the sea; the early Bronze Age Dromberg Stone Circle.

Food and Drink

① CUCINA

9 Market Street, Kinsale; tel: 021-470 0707; www.cucina.ie; B, L and AT; €

The best cappuccino in town is served in a smartly designed contemporary café. Daily specials – paninis, pastas and salads – are light and imaginative, using, for example, goat's cheese, rocket and local charcuterie.

② THE PINK ELEPHANT

Harbour View, Kilbrittain; tel: 023-884 9608; June–Sept daily L and D, May and Oct Thur–Fri D, Sat–Sun L and D, rest of year tel to confirm; €–€€

Midway between Kinsale and Timoleague, this bar-restaurant has an unforgettable view across the Atlantic. By day, freshly prepared light meals can be enjoyed at outdoor tables. Substantial portions of steak, lamb and imaginatively prepared local fish feature on the unpretentious dinner menu.

③ HAYES' BAR

The Square, Glandore; tel: 028-33214; daily B, L and D, Oct–May Sat–Sun only; €

This simple local pub has a superb bay view and offers a surprising range of wines by the glass. Local prawns, crab and salmon are served in open sandwiches and West Cork farmhouse cheese features in the croque monsieur. Tapas are served until 9pm.

on top of a cliff, nicknamed 'Million-aire's Row'. There is a magical view over a pair of islands to the open sea beyond. In sunny weather it is hard to resist an outdoor drink; try **Hayes' Bar**, see ⑪③ *(p.53)*.

ROARINGWATER BAY

The bay covers an area between the Mizen Head in the west and Balti-more in the east, and is known for its numerous rocks and islands. Its most famous landmark is the Fastnet Rock Lighthouse (the furthest point out from the start, in Cowes, England, of the tough yacht race that takes place every two years), which can be seen on the horizon some 23km (14 miles) to the south.

Skibbereen

Follow the narrow road through Glandore along the wooded estuary, rejoining the N71 at Leap. Continue west to **Skibbereen** ❻, a small market town, once a major junction on the West Cork Railway. The tiny **Skibbereen Heritage Centre** (Upper Bridge Street; tel: 028-40900; www.skibbheritage.com; mid-May–mid-Sept daily 10am–6pm, mid-Sept–mid-May Tue–Sat; charge) explains the Great Famine of 1845–9 *(see feature box, below)*, which took the lives of over 10,000 people locally. It is narrated by part-time local resident, Jeremy Irons. The centre also has a display on the Lough Hyne Marine Reserve, a saltwater lake nearby supporting unique forms of marine life.

Famine Food

The potato took very little labour to produce, allowing a farmer to feed his family, and also work for cash to pay the rent. A family of six could be fed for a year on 0.4 hectares (1 acre) of potatoes. By 1845 the population of Ireland had grown to 8 million, with the poorest totally dependent on the potato. When a fungus caused repeated crop failure between 1845 and 1849, about 2 million people died of starvation, cholera and dysentery. Another 2 million emigrated. Neither local land-lords nor the British government took responsibility for the situation. In west Cork so many people were competing for so little food it is said there was not a scrap of seaweed left on the coast from Baltimore to Ballydehob. Even today, the older generation refuses to eat mussels or other shellfish, referring to them as 'famine food'.

Baltimore

Baltimore ⑦ is the end of the road, so a visit from Skibbereen involves an optional 26km (16-mile) round trip on the R595. Baltimore was the original site of the English settlement in this area, but in 1631 Barbary pirates captured 107 inhabitants of the village ino slavery. The remaining English settlers moved inland to Skibbereen to escape further raids.

Baltimore is busy in July and August, when visiting yachts and other watersports enthusiasts join the local fleet of traditional wooden boats; boatbuilding is one of the most important local trades. Its one main street commands a glorious view of the harbour, and has a lively pub and café scene. Baltimore is the departure point for **Cape Clear** (Cape Clear ferry tel: 028-391 530) and **Sherkin Island** (ferry tel: 028-20218).

Both islands have a shop, bars, restaurants and overnight accommodation. **Sherkin Island**, 10 minutes offshore, is 5km (3 miles) long and 2.4km (1.5 miles) wide, and has quiet walks along fuchsia-lined roads, and sheltered sandy beaches. Irish-speaking **Cape Clear** is a dramatic 45-minute boat ride, through the jagged rocks of the Gascanane Sound. It is Ireland's southernmost point and has a population of about 130. Its Bird Observatory frequently reports rare migrants and the arrival of large flocks.

Ballydehob

Now return to Skibbereen and take the R71. A few kilometres out of town, there is a layby with a wonderful view of Roaringwater Bay and the Fastnet rock. **Ballydehob** ⑧ is a brightly painted hill village, a popular retreat for city folk – English, Dutch, German and even Irish – seeking a better quality of life. There is a pleasant walk centred on the old railway viaduct. (The railway line was closed as far back as 1947.)

Schull

While Ballydehob has a reputation as artistic, **Schull** ⑨ is the heart of fashionable west Cork, a summer resort for wealthy Dubliners and London media folk. Walk down to the pier to appreciate its waterside location, then explore its one main street (**T.J. Newmans**, see ⑪④, is an ideal spot for a break), which has lively bars and boutiques, an excellent bookshop and even a French *chocolatier*.

Food and Drink 🍴

④ T.J. NEWMAN'S
Main Street, Schull; tel: 028-27776; daily B, L and D; €
Instead of the traditional pub promised by the wooden façade, this is a sophisticated café-style restaurant, with a short but interesting menu showcasing local seafood and artisan produce, and a choice of 16 wines by the glass.

Above from far left:
Charles Fort *(see p.50)*; Skibbereen; gull out at sea near Schull.

Lighthouse Visit
If you like lighthouses, detour 14.5km (9 miles) southwest from Schull on the R592 to the Mizen Head Visitor Centre (tel: 028-35115: www. mizenhead.net; mid-Mar–Oct daily 10am–5pm, June–Aug until 6pm, winter Sat–Sun 11am–4pm only; charge). The centre is in the lighthouse keeper's house on an island at the tip of the rocky peninsula, accessed by a suspension bridge above a deep rocky chasm.

BANTRY BAY

Begin with a leisurely drive around the Sheep's Head, Cork's smallest, most undeveloped peninsula, before exploring the splendour of Bantry House and Gardens. View Bantry Bay and its neighbouring mountains from a height, before descending to the sheltered waters and lush vegetation of Glengarriff.

Coastal Walk
The Sheep's Head Way, a 100km (62-mile) walking route with sections sign-posted as loop walks, will lead you to megalithic remains, blowholes and other discoveries: pick up a brochure locally.

DISTANCE 90km (66 miles)
TIME A full day
START Durrus
END Glengarriff
POINTS TO NOTE
A car is essential for this tour. Friday is market day in Bantry, and the biggest market is on the first Friday of the month. Adrigole, the starting point of tour 7, the Ring of Beara, is 17km (10 miles) southwest of Glengarriff. Killarney, the start of tour 8, is 60km (37 miles) north of Glengarriff, via Kenmare (27km/16 miles). Kenmare has a better choice of restaurants and accommodation than Glengarriff or Bantry.

Bantry Bay is one of the great sights of western Ireland and the views from the vantage points on this tour are breathtaking. No less impressive are the gardens that lie along the way, from a memorial to an air disaster to a well-laid-out formal arrangement that perfectly complements the grand house to which it is attached.

SHEEP'S HEAD

The Sheep's Head peninsula, also known as Muntervary, is a finger of land dividing Dunmanus Bay from its bigger neighbour, Bantry Bay. Inhabited since megalithic times, it is a land of small farms with big sea views.

Durrus

Durrus ❶ is a village at the top of Dunmanus Bay where the road from the Mizen Head meets the road from the Sheep's Head. **The Sheep's Head Bar and Restaurant** (tel: 027-67878) does bar food all year round, but if the **Good Things Café**, see ⓘ①, is open, try that for its great food.

As you drive west along the sheltered inlet, past **St James' Church of Ireland** (1792), you can see the Mizen Head across the bay.

Air India Memorial

The **Air India Memorial** ❷, about 12km (8 miles) west of Durrus, is a peaceful waterside garden commemorating the 392 people who died on 23 June 1985 when an Air India flight was destroyed by a bomb. Many

of the bodies came ashore near here. Every year there is a memorial ceremony, and the sun hits the sundial in the garden at the exact moment of the explosion.

Rossnacaheragh Stone Circle

Park in **Ahakista** ❸ on the bend beyond the Ahakista Bar – known as the Tin Pub because of its corrugated-iron roof, a common replacement for thatch here. Follow the signpost for the Old Kilcrohane Road and walk up it about 10m/yds to a sign for the **Rossnacaheragh Stone Circle**. A flagstone path climbs uphill beside a pretty stream leading to a raised site with a small circle of megalithic stones. As usual, the view from the site is superb. The unpaved road below continues for another 400m/yds, passing a paddock of donkeys and a farmhouse.

Above from far left: Sheep's Head peninsula; Bantry Bay.

Food and Drink

① GOOD THINGS CAFÉ AND COOKERY SCHOOL

Ahakista Road, Durrus; tel: 027-61426; www.thegoodthingscafe.com; L, D July and Aug, Easter week, rest of year D Fridays, but tel to confirm. €€
This spare modern restaurant, run by Carmel Somers, disciple of English cookery writer Jane Grigson, is a mecca for foodies who love Carmel's simple way with local produce. Her creations include Swiss chard pizza with nutmeg and Durrus cheese.

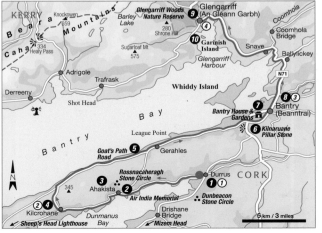

Whiddy Island

The largest island in Bantry Bay, Whiddy Island, is still inhabited by about six families, and accessible by a 10-minute ferry ride (tel: 027-50310) from the pier in Bantry Town. It is a peaceful spot for a gentle walk, with two lakes, abundant wild flowers and dramatic views of the mountains surrounding Bantry Bay. There is one pub-café, and hardly any traffic.

Kilcrohane

Return to your car and follow the main road for about 10km (6 miles) to **Kilcrohane ❹**. This is the biggest village (not counting Durrus) on the Sheep's Head, with three bars, a grocery shop, a petrol pump and a post office (the last three all one establishment, as in the old days). In summer there is a choice of restaurants, but turn right at the church, and you can get sandwiches all year round at **Fitzpatrick's Pub**, known as **Eileen's**, see ⑪②.

The Goat's Path

Thrill seekers may want to push on for another 12km (8 miles), on an ever-smaller road to the **Sheep's Head Lighthouse**, where there is rugged scenery, a car park and café, but the main tour takes the **Goat's Path ❺** for 19km (12 miles) to Bantry. (The Goat's Path is indeed more suitable for goats than cars; if you dislike driving along narrow roads with unfenced sheer drops, return to Bantry via Durrus.)

The Goat's Path starts beside Eileen's pub, and crosses to the northwest coast of the peninsula, past two viewing points. Here, on this more exposed shore, are stark cliffs and a different microclimate; the fuchsia hedges and orange montbretia of the south coast are replaced by ling, heather and gorse. There are no villages on this side, and there are fewer, more widely scattered houses, snugly built into sheltered spots between the hills.

Pillar Stone

Where the road joins the N71 turn left for Bantry and immediately right at the West Lodge Hotel to the **Kilnaruane Pillar Stone ❻** (free). The stone is indicated by a green and white fingerpost, and accessed by a galvanised gate. You will not see it until you reach the top of the field. The Pillar Stone is an early Christan pillar about 1.5m (5ft) high, dating from the 9th century, and carved with figurative and interlaced panels. When you have had a look, turn northwest for a breathtaking view of Bantry Bay and Whiddy Island: as so often at these sites, the view is every bit as rewarding as the antiquity.

BANTRY BAY

The bay is about 34km (21 miles) long and 6.5km (4 miles) wide. It was twice entered by French fleets attempting to invade Ireland, first in 1689, to aid James II, and again in 1796 when 14,000 troops, led by General Hoche, and the Irish patriot Wolfe Tone, were defeated by storms.

Bantry House and Gardens

Return to the main road, and turn right heading about 200m/yds to the shore of Bantry Bay and the car park for **Bantry House and Gardens ❼** (tel: 027-50047; www.bantryhouse.ie; Mar–Oct daily 10am–6pm; charge), which is set on a height overlooking the wide

Untimely Death
The writer J.G. Farrell, who won the 1973 Booker Prize for his novel *The Siege of Krishnapur*, and the 'Lost Booker' in 2010 for his Irish novel, *Troubles*, moved to the Kilcrohane area in 1979. He was swept to his death by a freak wave while fishing from the rocks near his house, and is buried at St James' Church, Durrus. A plaque commemorates him on the rocks on the north side of Sheep's Head Way near Carac Cairn.

bay and the surrounding mountains. The large mid-18th-century mansion is well worth a visit. Its interior contains a fine selection of treasures brought back by the first Earl of Bantry from his Grand Tour of Europe in the early 19th century, while the extensive garden has steep stone terraces, formal parterres, and a walled garden.

Bantry Town

It's a two-minute drive to **Bantry** **❽**, a quiet seaport and market town with a population of about 3,000, at the southeastern corner of the bay. The rafts that you see on the bay are evidence of the biggest local industry: mussel farming. You can sample the product in town at **O'Connor's Seafood Restaurant**, see 🍴③.

Glengarriff and Garinish Island

Beyond Bantry, the N71 runs along the water's edge through wooded **Ballylickey**, rising to a height above Bantry Bay, where there are several viewing points. Then it's downhill again to **Glengarriff ❾**, a sheltered inlet at the top of the bay with a subtropical climate. The harbour here is presided over by the **Eccles Hotel**, see 🍴④.

Continue into the village and park near Quills Woollen Mills. Beside the public toilets is a kiosk selling tickets for boat trips from the Blue Pool ferry point. Choose between an hour-long harbour trip, with close-up views of basking seals, or a visit to **Garinish**

Island ❿ (also known as Illnacullin; tel: 027-63040; www.heritageireland.ie; Apr–Sept Mon–Sat 10am–6.30pm, Sun 1–6.30pm, June–Aug Sun from 11am, Oct Sun 1–5pm; entry charge in addition to ferry; café), 10 minutes offshore. In the early 20th century part of the island was transformed into a series of gardens, using unusual shrubs and rare subtropical flowers.

For a scenic walk, drive through the busy village to **Glengarriff Woods Nature Reserve** (www.npws.ie), where there are a number of trails.

Food and Drink

② FITZPATRICKS'S PUB/EILEEN'S
Kilcrohane, Sheep's Head Peninsula; tel: 027-67057; sandwiches from 11am; €
Sometimes the 'craic' matters more than the food. It would be a sin not to sample this congenial pub, run according to her own rules (sandwiches only) by Eileen. Hikers gather at the outside table, and in winter there is a fire. The banter, encouraged by Eileen, is nonstop.

③ O'CONNOR'S SEAFOOD RESTAURANT
The Square, Bantry; tel: 027-50221; www.oconnorseafood.com; Mon–Wed and Sat D, Thur–Fri L and D; €€–€€€
This superb town-centre restaurant offers up a shoal of seafood delights, including chowder, oysters, calamari, fresh lobster by weight and mussels prepared in three different ways. Meat eaters and vegetarians are catered for too.

④ ECCLES HOTEL
Glengarriff Harbour; tel: 027-63003; www.eccleshotel.com; B, L and D; €–€€
All kinds of notable writers have stayed here, from William Thackeray to W.B. Yeats to Virginia Woolf. The food is standard hotel/bar fare, but you should visit this large 250-year-old hotel for its splendid location overlooking Glengarriff Harbour and the atmosphere of Victorian grandeur that persists.

THE RING OF BEARA

There will be no tour buses holding up the traffic on this day-long drive around the Beara Peninsula, a mecca for walkers and cyclists. Hospitality is basic but warm, and sea views hover at every turn. Allihies, a copper mining village and artists' hideaway between sea and mountains, is a highlight.

Literary Links
Daphne du Maurier's historical novel *Hungry Hill* is based on a local family feud. James Lovelock lived in Adrigole while writing *Gaia: a New Look at Life on Earth*, the basis for Earth System Science. Pete McCarthy's droll account of his Irish travels peaks in his *McCarthy's Bar* books. The French novelist and controversialist, Michel Houellebecq, author of *Atomised*, lived for some years on Bere Island, where he owns a house.

DISTANCE 82km (51 miles)
TIME A full day
START Adrigole
END Derreen Gardens
POINTS TO NOTE

A car is essential for this tour as there is no appropriate public transport. The only bank is in Castletownbere; so stock up on cash there. If you are based in Kenmare, start the tour by driving to Lauragh, and taking the Healy Pass to Adrigole. Kenmare, where there is a good choice of restaurants and places to stay, is 16km (10 miles) northeast of Tuosist. Killarney, the start of tour 8, is 27km (16 miles) north of Kenmare.

Food and Drink

① MURPHY'S RESTAURANT

Main Street, East End, Castletownbere; tel: 027-70244; B, L, D until 9pm, daily June–Aug, Mon–Sat Sept–May; €
This family-friendly café-restaurant is a much-loved local institution. There's a children's menu, and a wine licence for their parents. Fish and meat are locally sourced by the owner-chef, and served in generous, fishermen's portions.

This day of coastal views is full of wild and wonderful landscapes dotted with the remains of copper mining dating from the Bronze Age onwards. A slightly more unusual site is that of a Buddhist retreat, but one that fits well with the surrounding mountains.

THE SOUTH COAST

The Beara Peninsula stretches for about 48km (30 miles) southwest from Glengarriff. The Caha and the Slieve Miskish mountains run down the centre of the peninsula, a largely uninhabited area. The Ring of Beara is on a narrow coastal plain, with views across Bantry Bay, and then out to the Atlantic. Photographers will insist on many stops. The Beara Way, a 208km (129-mile) walking route, runs parallel to this southern section of the road a little further inland.

Adrigole

Adrigole ❶ is a scattered settlement around the shores of a small bay, backed by **Hungry Hill** (684m/2,247ft). There is evidence of Bronze Age copper mining in the hill, and it has

one of the highest waterfalls in Ireland on its northwest slope. A finger post by the road side indicates the footpath for a closer view of the waterfall.

Bere Island

Bere Island ❷ is about 10km (6 miles) long and 4km (2½ miles) wide, and lies 2km (1 mile) offshore. It has two regular ferry services, Murphy's from Pontoon (4km/2½ miles east of town; tel: 027-75014), and from Castletownbere (tel: 027-75009), both daily, year-round. The island forms a sheltered natural harbour, which remained in British hands until 1938. Some of the fortifications can still be seen. It is a quiet place of about 200 inhabitants, with an unspoilt environment, small coves for swimming, good walks and magnificent scenery.

Castletownbere

Castletownbere ❸, a busy fishing port with a population of about 900, is the biggest village on the peninsula. Get a feel for the place by walking along the quays and admiring the fishing fleet. Most of the buildings are in an imposing Victorian style, and date from the late 19th century when this was an important British naval base.

McCarthy's Bar *(see margin opposite)* on the main square has a grocery shop, which provisions the local trawlers. Across the road is **Murphy's Restaurant**, see ⍾①, where you can sample fresh local fish.

Dunboy Castle

Leave town on the R572, turning left after 5km (3 miles) at **Dunboy**, a small

Above from far left: colourful house in Eyeries; derelict cottage, Hungry Hill.

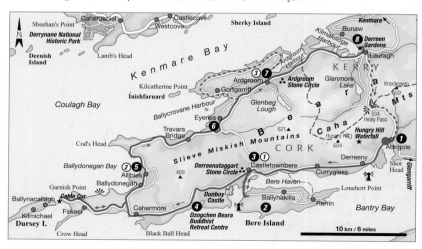

Megalithic Remains

The Beara is rich in megalithic and early Christian remains, and 25 of the best sites have been signposted from the public road, and parking spaces provided; pick up a leaflet at Beara Tourism, Church of Ireland, Castletownbere; tel: 027-70054; www. bearatourism.com. Among the most interesting are Derreenataggart Stone Circle at West End, Castletownbere, Kilcatherine Church and the Hag of Beara near Eyeries, and the Ardgroom Stone Circle.

wooded peninsula with waterside walks. Dunboy House, a stone mansion in the Scottish baronial style built by a copper magnate in the early 19th century, has been beautifully restored, and was due to open as a luxury hotel in 2007, but fell victim to the recession. Even as a shell, it is an impressive landmark, however, visible for many kilometres around.

Park nearby and walk to the tip of the peninsula to visit the weathered remains of the original Dunboy Castle, built in the 16th century by the O'Sullivan clan. They retreated here after defeat at the Battle of Kinsale in 1601, and blew it up rather than surrender to the English.

Buddhist Centre

As you continue west on the R572 the scenery starts to become really spectacular. For a closer look at the coast, turn off at the display of colourful Tibetan prayer flags for the **Dzogchen Beara Buddhist Retreat Centre** ❹ (Garranes, Allihies; tel: 027-73032; www.dzogchenbeara. org). The centre is under the spiritual guidance of Sogyal Rinpoche, author of the bestselling *The Tibetan Book of Living and Dying*. Visitors are welcome to enjoy the centre's amazing Atlantic view, and visit their cliff-top meditation garden. In summer there is a pleasant café. Visitors can join a guided meditation most days, but phone to confirm.

Allihies

About 3km (2 miles) beyond Dzogchen Beara is a signpost offering two routes to Allihies (allah-*hees*), 10km or 7km (6/4 miles). The longer option (an extra 3km/1 mile) allows you to visit Dursey Island, a small rocky island accessible only by cable car, mainly of interest to birdwatchers. On either route be prepared for some great seascapes. **Allihies** ❺ is a straggling line of brightly coloured cottages, originally built for copper miners. Today the village is augmented by replica cottages, holiday homes, but they blend in from a distance. **Ballydonegan**, the sandy beach below the village, was formed of spoil from the copper mines.

Copper Mine Museum

The **Allihies Copper Mine Museum** (tel: 027-73218; Mon–Fri 10am–5pm, Sat–Sun noon–5pm; café; charge) explains the history of mining hereabouts, from the Iron Age to the Cornish miners in the 19th century, and the mass exodus to Butte, Montana, when the mines closed in the 1950s. The material is beautifully presented in a converted church, and there are also exhibitions by the many artists living locally.

Charles Tyrrell, one of Ireland's leading abstract artists, and a longtime resident of Allihies, was a prime mover in the Museum project. A 10km (6-mile) heritage walking trail leads you from the Museum on a tour of

the abandoned mine workings, from which there are fine views.

Take a break at **O'Neill's Pub**, see ①②, located just up the road from the museum.

THE NORTH COAST

As you travel up the north coast of Beara, the neighbouring Iveragh Peninsula shelters the coast and, aided by the Gulf Stream, creates a mild, frost-free climate and rich vegetation.

Eyeries and Ardgroom

The twisting, switchback road between Allihies and **Eyeries** ❻ (eye-er-*ees*), another village of small, bright coloured houses, is one of the highlights of the Ring of Beara. Eyeries is so quirky and photogenic it has featured in several films, including *The Purple Taxi* (1977). The Iveragh Peninsula is clearly visible across the Kenmare River. About 3km (2 miles) north of Eyeries the Ring of Beara turns left for 15km (9 miles), a detour that will take you to **Kilcatherine**, an early Christian church, and a rock known as the **Hag of Beara**. It is a hair-raising drive on a steep narrow road; you may prefer to keep straight on for 7km (4½ miles) to **Ardgroom** ❼, a one-street village with good food at **The Village Inn**, see ①③. There's a relaxing walk (5km/3 miles loop) from the bridge beside the Holly Bar to **Glenbeg Lough**, an uncannily peaceful spot.

Kilmakillogue Harbour

Kilmakillogue Harbour is a sleepy place, where mussels are landed from the rafts out in **Kenmare Bay**, and there's a thriving salmon farm. It is chiefly known for its waterside pub, **The Pier House**, which most people find impossible to resist, especially on a sunny day.

Derreen Gardens

At the next crossroads follow the signpost for **Derreen Gardens** ❽ (Tuosist; tel: 064-83588; daily 10am–6pm, Apr–Oct; charge). The garden was planted 100 years ago on a sheltered peninsula that forms the northern side of Kilmakillogue Harbour. The woodland gardens run down to the water's edge and contain azaleas and rhododendrons, massive stands of bamboo and groves of New Zealand tree ferns.

Above from far left: the road to Ardgroom; Eyeries; bovine break.

The Healy Pass
To link the end of this tour with the start (at Adrigole), you can go via the Healy Pass in a route shown in a dotted red line on the map on p.61. Signposted (R574) in Adrigole at the beginning of the route, this 13km (8-mile)-long feat of engineering rises in a series of small, sharp hairpin bends to 334m (1,095ft) above sea level, crossing the peninsula via a pass in the Caha mountains. There is a spectacular viewing point about 5km (3 miles) from Adrigole.

Food and Drink

② O'NEILL'S PUB
Main Street, Allihies; tel: 027-73008; L, D daily Mar–Oct; €
O'Neill's has tables outside with idyllic views, but best of all (the tip of Beara has no restaurants) it serves hot food – six to eight blackboard items, daily roast, stews and steaks, open sandwiches and the catch of the day.

③ THE VILLAGE INN
Main Street, Ardgroom; tel: 027 74067; L, Mon–Sat, D 6–8.30pm Tue–Sun, book in advance for D July–Aug; €–€€
The enterprising landlords have a restaurant in an airy extension, and also serve food in the bar. A short menu of fresh local produce is prepared by the owner's son, a talented chef, and served by their daughter.

KILLARNEY

Killarney has a reputation for being a tourist trap, but its glorious countryside more than compensates. The romantic scenery of boulder-strewn, heather-clad mountains, lush vegetation, deep-blue lakes amid wild woodlands, all permeated by the aroma of peaty leaf mould, has an irresistible charm.

DISTANCE 82km (51 miles)
TIME One day, or a day and a half including the Gap of Dunloe
START Ladies' View
END Gap of Dunloe
POINTS TO NOTE
Killarney (www.killarney.ie) is accessible by rail from Dublin and Cork. If you are in Killarney without a car, visit Ross Castle on foot, take a jaunting car to Muckross Park, and an organised tour of the Gap of Dunloe. Alternatively, hire a bicycle and spend a day exploring the southern trail. Killorglin, the starting point of tour 9, is 13km (8 miles) west of Beaufort.

Dung-Free

In May 2010, Killarney's jarveys (Irish jaunting-car drivers) lost their High Court challenge to a ban on driving through Muckross Park unless they agreed to attach dung-catchers (aka horse nappies) to their jaunting cars. The jarveys feared the devices would make their horses bolt. The Minister for the Environment applauded the result, saying that a 'dung-free landscape' could only add to visitors' enjoyment.

Killarney's National Park, the focus of this tour, has no boundaries or entrance gates, but is a designated area of 10,000 hectares (25,000 acres), encompassing the three lakes of Killarney, and much of the mountains and woods that surround them. At its core is Muckross Park, an estate bordering on the Middle Lake and Lough Leane.

THE SOUTHERN TRAIL

Try to arrive in Killarney on the N71 road from Glengarriff and Kenmare. This mountain road passes through a series of short rock tunnels, while sheep graze in sparsely inhabited valleys. The first view of Killarney's chain of lakes running through a rocky, partially wooded valley is at Moll's Gap (500m/1,600ft). Stop about 3km (2 miles) further on at **Ladies' View** ❶, where you will be looking north on to the lakes, with the hills known as the Macgillycuddy's Reeks in the west.

Torc Waterfall

The road winds down the hill, entering an area of ancient oak forest, with rich undergrowth of hazel, typical of Killarney's woodlands. Stop 10km (6 miles) further on at the **Torc Waterfall** ❷ car park, and climb the path and steps by the waterfall. It is at its best after a period of heavy rain, when it has a wonderful damp woodland aroma.

Muckross Park

Continue for another 3km (1.8 miles) on the N71 to the main entrance

of **Muckross Park** (free parking). **Muckross House** ❸ (tel: 064-663 1440; daily, Sept–June 9am–5.30pm, July–Aug 9am–7pm; last admission one hour before closing; charge) is an Elizabethan-style mansion dating from 1843, with formal gardens, and can be visited on guided tours. The **Visitor Centre** (hours as house, Nov-mid-Mar on request; free) next door has leaflets on the park's walking trails, an audiovisual presentation and other information. The best option is **Muckross Traditional Farms** (hours as Muckross House, but mid-Mar–Apr, Sat–Sun and holidays 1–6pm), a walking trail of about 2km (1 mile) visiting three different working farms of the pre-electricity era (a complimentary coach operates for non-walkers, but confirm in advance), complete with Kerry cows and a pair of Irish wolfhounds. The costumed 'farmers' and their 'wives' are not actors, but knowledgeable experts on their topics, and you will enjoy an informative chat.

There is a circular walk of about 6km (4 miles) from Muckross House around the Middle Lake to the **Meeting of the Waters**; ask for a leaflet or follow the signs.

Above from far left: bakery in Killarney; bridled horses at Muckross House.

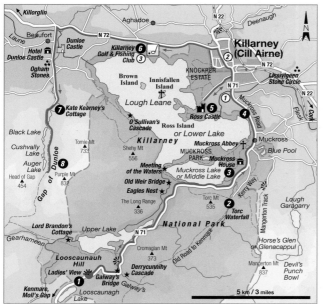

Kerry Cows
The black Kerry cow, a small cow by modern standards, is a docile creature with a long pedigree, said to be the oldest in Europe, in existence since 4,600BC. Ireland has a national herd of 6.1 million cows, but only 500 are Kerry cows. They can be seen in Killarney National Park, and are also bred by enthusiasts in other parts of Kerry.

Above: abbey remains on Innisfallen Island; looking over the atmospheric lake.

Jaunting Tours

The second entrance to Muckross House (previous page), nearer to the town, is reserved for pedestrians and traditional jaunting cars, an open pony and trap driven by 'jarveys' some of whom include a commentary on the experience. They cost €40 an hour for up to four people, but on a quiet day you can try to strike a bargain. Alternatively, pre-book a jaunting car to collect you from your accommodation (Tangney Tours; tel: 064-663 3358; www.killarney jauntingcars.com).

Muckross Road

The N71 is now known as **Muckross Road ❹** and is the location of some of Killarney's biggest hotels. The Lake Hotel was built as a lakeside residence in 1820; Queen Victoria stayed here on her 1861 visit, while The Gleneagle has Ireland's largest conference venue, and is also used for big-name entertainment acts. Just before crossing the River Flesk to Killarney town, turn left at the sign for the **Cahernane House Hotel**, see ⑪①, one of the most elegant country-house hotels in Killarney. Between here and Killarney town the road is lined with modern B&Bs.

Ross Castle

After the first traffic light at the entrance to town, look out for a signpost on the left for a 3.4km (1.5-mile) detour to **Ross Castle ❺** (tel: 064-663 5851; daily, but closed Mon mid-Oct–mid-Nov; charge), an impressive lakeside stronghold built by the O'Donoghue Ross chieftains in the mid-15th century, with later additions. It is furnished with 16th- and 17th-century oak. You can hire a boat here and take a picnic over to **Innisfallen Island** about 2km (1 mile) offshore, or travel on the covered-in motor launch that runs hourly (Billy Tangney, tel: 087-257 1492; charge).

The wooded island has the remains of an abbey founded in about AD600. The early Irish monks had a great eye for a beautiful location, and could be said to have been the first to discover the pleasures of Killarney.

NORTH AND WEST OF KILLARNEY

Beaufort, a village northwest of Killarney's lakes, is the starting point for the Gap of Dunloe, a scenic mountain pass. The terrain is harsh on this side, bare mountains slopes with none of the lush vegetation of the south. You can travel from the Gap back to Killarney by jaunting car and boat, a day-long trip, and return by coach to your car, or book the trip in reverse in Killarney. Others opt to walk only halfway down the Gap, and return to their car. A useful stop in Killarney is **Treyvaud's**, see ⑪②.

Killarney Golf and Fishing Club

Leave Killarney town on the N72, signposted Killorglin. About 3km (2 miles) down the road is **Killarney Golf and Fishing Club ❻** (Mahony's Point; tel: 064-663 1034) which has three golf courses in stunning lake and mountain scenery, and has hosted the Irish Open three times. The bar, see ⑪③, is open to non-golfers. The Club opened in 1939. Like much of Killarney's tourism development from the same era, it aimed to create jobs in a depressed rural economy.

Dunloe Castle

Head west again on the N72 and continue for another 6.5km (4 miles).

The **River Laune**, which joins the lakes to the sea, and is one of Ireland's finest salmon rivers, runs parallel to the road. After about 6.5km (4 miles) you reach the left fork for the Gap of Dunloe. The gates of **Hotel Dunloe Castle** are on the right about 1.6km (1 mile) down the road. Now a luxury hotel, there is public access to the remains of the original 13th-century castle. Walk down the gravel path to the left of the entrance for about five minutes through well-tended gardens. The castle is above the River Laune. A romantic ruin with flowers and trees growing from its ruined battlements, its river façade has a sensational group of nine wide lancet windows.

Kate Kearney's Cottage

Leave the hotel and head south for 1km (½ mile), parking at **Kate Kearney's Cottage 7**. It is now a tourist-orientated bar-restaurant, but in the early 19th century it was the cabin of a great beauty who sold 'mountain dew', or poteen (illegally distilled whiskey), to thirsty tourists. Jaunting cars can be hired here, to drive halfway down the Gap, or you can walk. You can also take a guided tour *(see above right)*.

Gap of Dunloe

About forty families live in the Black Valley, and have car access to the road; everyone else must walk. Once you turn your back on the tourist paraphernalia around the car park, the **Gap of Dunloe 8** is a great way to experience the mountains, and see those boulders, mossy hags and gorse bushes close to. The gap narrows between the steep slopes of Purple Mountain (832m/2,770ft) which looms up on the left. Most people turn back at this point, but for reference the route (11.5km/7 miles in total) continues to the south shore of the Upper Lake (13km/8 miles southwest of Killarney), from where you can proceed by boat through the three lakes to Ross Castle. (Tours leave Kate Kearney's Cottage daily at 11am, and return by 4.30pm; tel: 064-663 0200.)

Above from far left: Muckross House; Gap of Dunloe; Kate Kearney's Cottage.

Food and Drink

① CAHERNANE HOUSE HOTEL
Muckross Road, Killarney; tel: 064-663 1895; L, D; €€
The trees meet overhead on the approach to this imposing Victorian country house, a perfect refuge from the tourist trail. It looks very expensive, but the Cellar Bar, in a cleverly converted wine cellar, serves salads, sandwiches and light lunches that will not break the bank.

② TREYVAUD'S
62 High Street, Killarney; tel: 064-663 3062; Wed–Sun, Oct–Apr, L, D; €–€€€
A lively contemporary town-centre restaurant, this is the place to go when the outdoor air has sharpened your appetite. At lunch try beef and Guinness pie with mashed potato, while the dinner menu has more adventurous options, including locally farmed ostrich. Known for game in winter.

③ KILLARNEY GOLF AND FISHING CLUB
Mahony's Point, Killarney; tel: 064-31034; Mon–Sat, L, D; €€
You won't forget you're in Killarney at the clubhouse's upstairs restaurant, superbly located on Lough Leane. The large U-shaped room has panoramic views on three sides. Choose from the all-day menu, or blackboard specials, which include salads as well as hearty golfer's fare.

THE RING OF KERRY

The Ring of Kerry is one of Europe's great scenic drives, a circular route around the rim of the Iveragh Peninsula, through rugged sandstone hills and verdant subtropical vegetation, with myriad mountain and coastal views.

DISTANCE 140km (87 miles)

TIME 1 or 2 days

START Killorglin

END Kenmare

POINTS TO NOTE

A car is essential to tour the Ring independently. Tour bus traffic leaves Killarney 16km (10 miles) east of Killorglin between 9am and 10am travelling anticlockwise, so leave earlier or later. Showery weather can add dramatic light effects, but if the forecast is for heavy rain, make other plans. Allow two days if you intend to visit the Skellig Rocks, a 3- to 4-hour boat trip; book ahead and bear in mind that the ferry leaves Portmagee at 10.30am.

Perfect Beach

From Cahirciveen, drive straight on at the Barracks to the bridge, and go 'over the water', as they say locally, to a small, sparsely populated peninsula. At this point, turn left. Here, the road passes a 6th-century stone fort (free). Signs for *Trá* (Irish for beach) lead to White Strand, an idyllic little Blue Flag beach sheltered from the prevailing winds, overlooking Valentia Island. Don't forget your picnic.

Food and Drink

① CAMO'S CAFÉ AND RESTAURANT

Church Street, Cahirciveen; tel: 066-948 1122; daily B and L, June–Aug also D; €

Talented owner-chef, Rory McCarthy, provides tasty fare at this simple café opposite the church. Relax in a window seat and sample an open fresh prawn sandwich and home-made lemon meringue pie.

The Ring of Kerry follows the coast of the Iveragh Peninsula in the extreme southwest. The route overlooks Dingle Bay to the north, the open Atlantic to the west and the sheltered waters of Kenmare Bay to the south. Inland, to the east, are the purple hills known as Macgillycuddy's Reeks and the Lakes of Killarney *(see p.64)*. The Gulf Stream ensures a mild, frost-free climate.

DINGLE BAY

At **Killorglin ❶** on the River Laune join the Ring of Kerry (N70) by driving west across the river and up the steep main street. This market town is known for its annual Puck Fair (www.puckfair.ie), a street festival held in August.

Kerry Bog Village Museum

The scenery begins to live up to expectations about 8km (5 miles) beyond Killorglin amid wild, sparsely inhabited hills. Stop at the Red Fox Inn for the **Kerry Bog Village Museum ❷** (tel: 066-976 9184; www.kerrybog village.ie; Mar–Nov daily 8.30am– 7pm; charge), three reconstructed cottages with turf fires, ponies and

dogs. It commemorates the simple rural lifestyle that persisted locally until the mid-20th century.

Rossbeigh

Just beyond tiny **Glenbeigh**, detour 2km (1¼ miles) on the R564 to **Rossbeigh ❸**, a 6.5km (4-mile) sandy beach facing north across Dingle Bay. Take a few minutes to get your bearings and enjoy the sea air. After Glenbeigh the road curves dramatically towards the coast, following a cliff top between the mountains and the pounding Atlantic.

Cahirciveen

Cahirciveen ❹ is the chief market town of south Kerry, but usually has a deserted air, even over 150 years after being devastated by the Famine.

Park near the **Tourist Information Office** (Church Street; tel: 066-947 2589) and walk down the side road to the **Old Barracks** (tel: 066-947 2777; Mon–Fri 10am–4.30pm, Sat 11.30am–4.30pm, Sun 1–5pm; charge), an exotic white turreted building that once housed the local constabulary. Restored as a Heritage Centre, it has informative displays on local history, including the Famine. From here, you can see the estuary of the Carhen River, the more attractive side of town. Back at the main road turn west to the **O'Connell Memorial Church**, a huge Gothic-style edifice with a black limestone façade, built in 1888. Across the road is **Gallery One**, showcasing the work of the local craft cooperative, and **Camo's**, see ⑪①, a good spot for a break.

Above from far left: panoramic view of the Ring of Kerry; O'Connells from Cahirciveen include the politician Daniel (1775–1847; *see p.72*), who campaigned for Catholic Emancipation (the right to sit in Parliament).

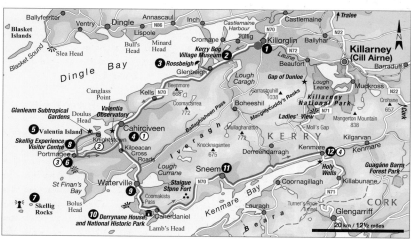

ATLANTIC COAST

The area between Valentia Island and Derrynane looks straight out to the Atlantic, and lacks the shelter provided to the other two coasts by neighbouring peninsulas. Consequently the wind can be stronger hereabouts.

Valentia Island

As you leave Cahirciveen, the **Valentia Observatory**, now part of the Irish meteorological service, is on the right. It was originally (from 1868) sited on **Valentia Island ⑤**, because the island had a telegraphic link to London and was in the path of most weather systems coming in from the Atlantic.

Between April and September (when the ferry runs), turn right at Reenard Cross for the **Valentia Island Ferry** (tel: 066-947 6141; daily 8.15am–10pm; charge) to **Knightstown**. Outside ferry months, shortly beyond the Observatory, head west for 12km/7½ miles to Portmagee, cross the causeway and drive up the island for 11.5km/7 miles to Knightstown.

Knightstown, which was built for the workers at the Cable Station and the Observatory, is like a little bit of England, with terraces of solidly built white-painted houses lining the waterfront, an ornate Clock Tower and the Royal Hotel (nowadays a hostel and pub). If you are looking for food, walk a short step up the village's one inland-facing street to **Fuchsia Restaurant**,

see ⑪②. Valentia has a population of about 500, and is around 11km (7 miles) long and 3km (2 miles) wide. There is good walking on quiet roads, with a wealth of sea views. Valentia is also famous for its slate, which is of great density and hardness, and was used to roof the Palace of Westminster and the Paris Palais Garnier opera house. The main quarry was abandoned after a rock fall, but is worth visiting for its wonderful sea views. It is referred to locally as 'the grotto', as statues of the Virgin Mary and St Bernadette were somehow erected high on its façade during the Marian Year, 1952.

Glanleam Subtropical Gardens (tel: 066-947 6176; Apr–Oct daily 10am–7pm; charge) are about 1.6km (1 mile) from Knightstown in a sheltered waterside location. The garden was originally planted in the 1850s, and is beautifully maintained by its current owners. Tree ferns, bamboo groves, cordylines, azaleas and other exotic plants thrive in the frost-free climate. Allow a couple of hours to see it all.

After leaving the gardens, drive south on the R565 to Portmagee.

Portmagee and Skellig Rocks

If the ferry is not running, shortly beyond the observatory, head west for 12km (7½ miles) to **Portmagee ⑥**, a tiny fishing village and the departure point for the boat trip to Skellig Rocks. **The Bridge Bar** here is perfect for a bowl of seafood chowder, see ⑪③.

Above: cows enjoying the Irish countryside; fishing kit at Portmagee; Ring of Kerry views.

Valentia's Name

The name Valentia comes from the Irish name for the channel between the island and the mainland, Beale Inse, and has nothing to do with Spain's Valencia.

Weather permitting, small open boats make the 13km (8-mile) crossing from Portmagee to **Skellig Rocks** ❼ (leaves 10.30am; tel: 066-947 6214; www.skelligsrock.com) in about an hour. Little Skellig is home to over 27,000 gannets, while the Unesco-listed Skellig Michael (where landing is permitted) rises to a double peak 217m (712ft) high. Over 500 stone steps lead to a simple monastery, its dry-stone buildings clinging to the cliff-edge, as they have done since the 7th century.

If you are unable to take the boat trip, drive across the causeway to Valentia Island to visit the **Skellig Experience Visitor Centre** ❽ (tel: 066-947 6306; www.skelligexperience.com; Apr–Nov daily 10am–6pm; charge), which introduces visitors to the history and wildlife of Skellig Michael and the other rocks.

Waterville

Return to the main ring road and drive south 11km (7 miles) to **Waterville** ❾, a small resort famous for its golf course and the game angling on Lough Currane. Park in the centre near the Butler Arms and statue of Charlie Chaplin, who used to holiday here regularly. Take a walk on the windswept sandy beach to see if you share his enthusiasm.

Derrynane House

Stop at the parking area on the **Coomakista Pass** to enjoy impressive views of the Skelligs to the west and the mountains of the Beara Peninsula to the south.

In Caherdaniel drive downhill to **Derrynane House and National Historic Park** ❿ (tel: 066-947 5113; www.heritageireland.ie; May–Sept Mon–Sat 9am–6pm, Sun 11am–7pm, Apr and Oct Tue–Sun 1–5pm, Nov–Mar Sat–Sun 1–5pm; charge), family home of Daniel O'Connell *(see p.72)*. The modest 1702 manor house is furnished with heirlooms. Walk along the sheltered beach and explore the rock pools.

(see p.72)

Above from far left: views of Valentia Island *(far left* and *centre);* the beach at Waterville.

Food and Drink 🍴

② FUCHSIA RESTAURANT AND COURTYARD

Market Street, Knightstown, Valentia Island; tel: 066 847 6051; D June–Sept Wed–Sun, rest of year D Fri–Sun, closed Bank Holidays and 2 weeks at Christmas; €€
You dream of finding a place like this after a day outdoors: tasty, freshly prepared food served in a stylishly converted shop with fuchsia-pink walls. The hake-bake is a must, the lamb shank cannot be faulted, and the desserts are divine.

③ THE BRIDGE BAR

Portmagee; tel: 066-947 7108; www.moorings.ie; daily L and D, Oct–Apr no food served on Mon; €
Located right on the seafront, with a rustic pine interior warmed by an open fire. The simply prepared fish is leaping fresh; alternatively, opt for the roast of the day.

Above: street in Kenmare; boats moored near Dingle.

The Liberator

Daniel O'Connell (1775–1847), 'the Liberator', was born in Cahirciveen and adopted by an uncle, from whom he inherited an estate at Derrynane. Landowner, lawyer and orator, he dominated Irish politics in the early 19th century. Educated in France (as were many wealthy Catholics), he was responsible for the Catholic Emancipation Act of 1829, allowing Catholics and Dissenters to vote, enter the professions and own land. Tall, burly and inexhaustible, O'Connell was famed for his huge appetite and physical stamina. He was no saint, though – he fought a fatal duel in his youth and had a reputation as a womaniser – but all this seemed to endear him all the more to the people. Most Irish towns and villages now have an O'Connell Street.

Food and Drink 🍽

④ THE PARK HOTEL

Kenmare; tel: 064-664 1200; www.parkkenmare.com; daily lounge noon–6pm, dining room D; €€–€€€€

Kenmare is the foodie capital of southwest Ireland, and the Park is the jewel in its crown. The elegant dining room, built in 1897 by the Great Southern Railway, is imposing but friendly. Food is light but flavoursome, featuring seafood and local specialities, such as Kerry lamb and Skeghanore duck. The bar and lounge serve a lighter menu during the day.

KENMARE RIVER

The Kenmare River is a sea inlet that divides the Iveragh Peninsula from the Beara Peninsula in the south.

Sneem

Brightly painted **Sneem** ⑪ has two village greens; park by the second. Walk down the road beyond the Blue Bull (signposted 'Pier') for about 300m/yds past the attractive **Garden of the Senses**. Looking back through the reeds you can appreciate Sneem's sheltered location between the sea and the hills. Note the difference in vegetation on this side of the Ring; in the place of bare windswept rocks is a lush growth of trees and shrubs. The large **Parknasilla Hotel** here has welcomed many celebrities and dignatories in its time, including George Bernard Shaw, Charlie Chaplin and Charles de Gaulle.

Kenmare

Follow the N70 east for 27km (17 miles) to **Kenmare** ⑫. Laid out in 1755 in a triangle, the compact village is packed with restaurants, boutiques and crafts shops. Park in its centre beside the green and the **Kenmare Heritage Centre** (tel: 064-664 1223), which introduces the town's history. There is a lively restaurant scene in Kenmare's centre, but for somewhere really memorable try **The Park Hotel**, see 🍽④, just outside of town, a left turn off the N71 towards Bantry.

THE DINGLE PENINSULA

Jutting out into the Atlantic, the Dingle Peninsula is Europe's most westerly point. The Irish-speaking area at its tip is rich in prehistoric and early Christian remains, and has rugged cliffs and sandy beaches. Finish by crossing the sensational Conor Pass to Camp.

Begin at Castlemaine, the southern gateway to the Dingle Peninsula (Corca Dhuibhne), which stretches for some 48km (30 miles) from Tralee in the east to Slea Head in the west.

CASTLEMAINE TO DINGLE

Some 10km (6 miles) beyond **Castlemaine ❶** the sea comes into view as the road skirts Castlemaine Harbour. The first hint of the spectacular scenery to come is at **Inch ❷**, where a 6.5km (4-mile) long sand spit backed by dunes stretches out into Dingle Bay. Stop for a bracing walk along the

DISTANCE 119km (67½ miles)
TIME A full day
START Castlemaine
END Camp
POINTS TO NOTE

All signposts to Dingle are in Irish: *An Daingean*. There is a daily bus service from Tralee to Dingle town, but a car is essential for this tour. Avoid the Conor Pass in misty weather; instead take the N86 to Camp. Note, there isn't a petrol station or ATM west of Dingle town. Tralee, *see tour 11*, is 13km (8 miles) east of Camp on the N86.

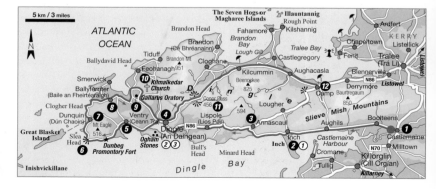

Above: cheeky gull.

Blasket Trips
Dunquin Pier is a steep concrete footpath that spirals down to the sea, where curraghs (canoes covered in tarred canvas) are stored upside down. A modern ferry (tel: 087-231 6131; www.blasketislands. ie) makes the 20-minute crossing to Great Blasket Island, weather permitting, up to eight times a day between Easter and October. Walk through the traffic-free island's deserted village and along narrow cliff paths rich in wildlife, and watch the seals on White Strand.

unusual west-facing beach and refuel at **Sammy's**, see ⑪①.

Annascaul

The wide road at **Annascaul ❸**, where the Castlemaine and Tralee roads meet, was once the location of a major cattle fair, which is also why this tiny village has so many pubs. One such pub, the **South Pole Inn** (tel: 066-915 2626), was built by Tom Crean (1877–1938), a local man of legendary strength who enlisted in the Royal Navy and served on three Antarctic expeditions, with both Scott and Shackleton. The pub is crammed with fascinating polar memorabilia, and you can enjoy a view of green hills and grazing sheep from its front door, as Crean must have on many a morning.

Dingle Town and Harbour

From Annascaul, it's 17km (10½ miles) west to **Dingle ❹** (An Daingean). Turn left at the entrance and park on the pier. Dingle has a population of about 1,500, which can treble in summer. Its fame was spread by the filming of *Ryan's Daughter* in 1969, and again in 1983 by the arrival of a dolphin, Fungie, who still plays in the harbour mouth. A bronze statue on the pier pays homage to the wild visitor.

Opposite, in a humble tin shed, is Dingle's best seafood restaurant, **Out of the Blue**, see ⑪②. A triangular 10-minute walk from the pier up

Green Street, down Main Street and back along the Mall will take you past most of the town's shops and restaurants. In Main Street is **Ashe's Bar**, see ⑪③. The best craft shops are at the top of Green Street.

Heading out of Dingle towards Slea Head, just beyond the marina you pass the **Oceanworld Mara Beo Aquarium** (The Wood, tel: 066-915 2111; daily from 10am–6pm; 5pm Nov–Mar; charge), where you can get up close to more than 100 species of live fish, from tiny native Irish sea horses to fearsome sand tiger sharks – this is a good rainy-day option to amuse the kids.

SLEA HEAD DRIVE

Head west for 6km (3¾ miles) on the R559 to **Ventry ❺** (Ceann Trá), an Irish-speaking village with a few pubs and shops. The bay here has a long sandy beach and safe swimming.

Between Ventry and Slea Head there are over 400 small conical huts of unmortared stone known as beehive huts. While some date from the 5th–8th centuries and were used by hermit monks, many were built in the early 20th century to house farm implements; timber is so scarce here that it is cheaper to build with stone.

Dunbeg Promontory Fort

About 6km (4 miles) further, stop at the distinctive Stone House Res-

taurant at **Fahan** to visit **Dunbeg Promontory Fort** (tel: 066-915 9755; www.dunbegfort.com; Apr–Oct daily 10am–5pm; charge), a defensive promontory fort that was inhabited around AD800–1200. Inside, a short film introduces visitors to the history of the compact site, which has an inner dry-stone rampart and a souterrain. It is perched right on the cliff's edge, reached by a short downhill path beside a field grazed by donkeys. About 250m/yds on, park again to visit a group of beehive huts above the road (charge). In fine weather you can look south across the sea to the Skellig Rocks (*see p.71, Ring of Kerry tour*), where hardy monks lived in similar shelters.

Slea Head

The road climbs west around Mt Eagle to **Slea Head ❻** (Ceann Sléibhe), marked by a life-size road-side Crucifixion. Coumenole, the sandy beach below, will be familiar to anyone who has seen the film *Ryan's Daughter*. It looks tempting, but swimming here is dangerous.

Dunquin and the Blasket Islands

Nearby **Dunquin ❼** (Dún Chaoin) is a scattered settlement, as was common in old Gaelic Ireland. The **Great Blasket** (An Blascaod Mór) is the largest of seven islands visible offshore. It was inhabited until 1953 by a tough, self-sufficient community of farmers and fishermen. The **Great Blasket Centre** (tel: 077-915 6444; www.heritage ireland.ie; daily 10am–6pm, July–Aug until 7pm; charge) at Dunquin explains the islanders' heritage. From **Dunquin Pier** you can catch a ferry to the island *(see margin opposite)*.

Gallarus Oratory

Continue on the R559 for 7km (4 miles) to Irish-speaking **Ballyferriter ❽** (Baile an Fheirtéaraigh), the largest village on this side of the peninsula (it has two shops and four pubs that serve simple food). Founded by the Norman Ferriter family in the 12th century, it

Above from far left: Slea Head; Dunbeg Fort; Out of the Blue does great seafood.

Food and Drink

① SAMMY'S STORE AND CAFÉ
Inch Beach; tel: 066-915 8118; daily B, L and D; €
Sammy's has an amazing location right on the beach, and has a child-friendly café as well as a bar. By day it serves simple but freshly prepared salads, burgers, soups and sandwiches, while at night the menu features fresh fish and steaks.

② OUT OF THE BLUE
The Pier, Dingle town; tel: 066-915 0811; Mon–Tue and Thur–Sun L and D; €€€
It's a basic tin hut beside the pier, but it serves the freshest of seafood. Lobster, John Dory, brill, black sole and even the humble mackerel appear on the daily specials blackboard, cooked to perfection in classic style with a modern twist. Book in advance to avoid disappointment.

③ ASHE'S BAR
Main Street, Dingle town; tel: 066-915 0989; www.ashes seafoodbar.com; daily L and D; €€
Ashe's pioneered bar food in Dingle, feeding the cast of *Ryan's Daughter* in 1969. It's a cosy, quirky, old-fashioned pub, but fear not, as the menu is bang up to date, with prawn tempura, grilled oysters, rib-eye steak and squid salad.

Ogham Stones
These are carved with
letters from the early
medieval Ogham
alphabet, in which
the letters are made
up of parallel lines
and notches.

is popular today with holiday-makers
and Irish-language enthusiasts.

Some 8km (5 miles) further on is
the **Gallarus Oratory** ❾ (visitor
centre: tel: 066-915 5333, charge;
oratory: free). This extraordinary 8th-
century building of unmortared stone
is shaped like an inverted boat, and is
still dry and solid.

At the crossroads north of Gallarus, turn right (east) for the ruined
Kilmalkedar Church ❿. It was built
around 1150, although the settlement dates from the 7th century. The
superbly carved Romanesque features
have hardly weathered over the years.
There are a number of interesting
standing stones nearby, including a
sundial stone and several Ogham
stones *(see margin, left)*.

CONOR PASS TO CAMP

Return to Dingle on the R559 (8km/
5 miles). If the weather is fine, drive
to Camp via the **Conor Pass** ⓫
(25km/16 miles), a rocky mountain
road that crosses the peninsula from
south to north. It rises steeply to 456m
(1,496ft) above sea level, and parts are
so narrow that you must negotiate right
of way with oncoming traffic. It is not
for the faint-hearted, but it does offer
spectacular vistas of Brandon Bay and
the wide Atlantic ocean in the north;
stop in a lay-by to enjoy the view. The
road then corkscrews down to the bay,
past a dazzling waterfall and boulder-
strewn hillsides studded with glittering
lakes. **Camp** ⓬ marks the end of the
scenic circuit of the Dingle Peninsula.

Right: detail of
the ruined Kilmalk-
edar Church.

TRALEE AND NORTH KERRY

After a look at Tralee's County Museum and town centre, follow a relaxing day-long drive visiting ecclesiastical remains and sandy beaches. Get lost in the dunes of Banna Strand, or soak in a seaweed bath at Ballybunion. Then head for Listowel, famous for poets, horse racing and its gastro-pub.

Between Tralee and the Shannon estuary the land is flat, with big skies, and predominantly agricultural. The area attracted monastic communities from early Christian times. Ballybunion and Listowel were the traditional places for farmers to relax after the harvest, and both have retained an old-fashioned charm.

TRALEE

Tralee, the administrative centre of Kerry, was founded in the 13th century by the Anglo-Normans. Modern Tralee took shape in the 19th century, when it gained a railway connection. The town also benefited from the economic boom of the late 20th century.

Kerry County Museum
Tralee ❶ (Trá Lí) has a population of 35,000, many of whom are students. Beside the town park, the Ashe Memorial Hall, an imposing neoclassical building, houses the **Tourist Information Office** (tel: 066-712 1288). Park near here and explore

on foot. Denny Street leads from the museum to the commercial centre and contains the best of Tralee's Georgian houses. For refreshment, try the **Denny Lane Café**, see ⑪① *(p.79)*, in a pedestrian lane off Denny Street.

NORTH KERRY COAST

This part of Ireland was an important area during early Christian times, and many of its religious sites date from 6th-century foundations.

Local History
In Tralee's tourist office is the Kerry County Museum (tel: 066-712 7777; www.kerrycountymuseum.ie; June–Aug daily 9.30am–5.30pm, Sept–May Tue–Sat only; charge), with a lively display of Kerry's history from ancient times.

DISTANCE 58km (36 miles)
TIME A full day
START Tralee
END Listowel
POINTS TO NOTE
A car is essential for this tour: you can drive (or take a bus) directly from Tralee to Listowel in about half an hour, but this tour follows the scenic coast road then north to Ballybunion before heading south to Listowel.

Ardfert

Leave Tralee on the R551 by driving west on Ivy Terrace in front of the museum, turning right at the T-junction, and taking the second left on Pembroke Street. On arriving at **Ardfert ❷** (9km/6miles), the one-way system will lead you to **Ardfert Cathedral** (tel: 066-713 4711; Easter and May–Sept daily 10am–6pm; free; visitor centre: charge). Originally founded in the 7th century by St Brendan the Navigator, the site consists of three medieval churches, of which the most memorable is the 13th-century cathedral with beautiful windows. Nearby, in a field surrounded by grazing cattle, are the remains of Ardfert Friary (free), founded in 1253.

Above: verdant countryside; signs in English and Irish.

Banna Strand

Return to the R551, and take the first left after about 1km (½ mile) for **Banna Strand ❸**. This is an 8km (5-mile) long sandy beach facing due west. The mountains of the Dingle Peninsula can be seen to the south. The dunes here rise to a height of 12m (40ft).

Turn south (left) to locate the memorial to Roger Casement (1864–1916), commemorating the landing of arms here in 1916 'to further Irish freedom', for which he was hung as a traitor by the British. Today this is a popular recreational area. If you keep walking or driving south, you will leave the caravan parks for less-frequented areas, and probably end up back in Ardfert: there are no signposts, but it is a beautiful place to wander.

Ballyduff

About 14km (8½ miles) north of Ballyheige, just outside **Ballyduff**, look out for a signpost for **Ratoo Round Tower ❹** (free) to the right. Drive past a couple of small farms for about 2km (1 mile) and park. There are the well-preserved remains of a small 15th-century church. Climb over the stile beside it to the round tower, one of Ireland's finest examples. It dates from the 10th century and is 27m (89ft) tall with a conical roof. The locked wooden door is about 3m (10ft) from the ground on the east, and there are four windows at the top facing the four points of the compass.

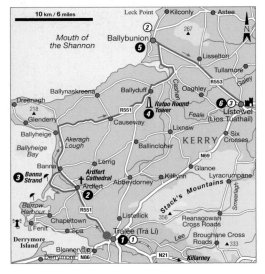

Ballybunion

Famous for its golf club, **Ballybunion 5**, 9km (5½ miles) north of Bally-duff, is a tiny village, surrounded by caravan parks and self-catering accommodation. Park centrally, and take the cliff walk, with views of the Men's and Ladies' Strands, the names a relic of segregated bathing that persisted into the 1930s. At **Ballybunion Seaweed Baths** (Ladies' Strand; tel: 068-27469; charge), individual bath tubs are filled with freshly picked seaweed and hot seawater, to ease your aches and pains. If all this activity has left you hungry, head to the cliff top in the village, and **The Bunker**, see ①②.

LISTOWEL

Listowel 6 is the only town in North Kerry, and is situated on the banks of the River Feale. It still has many original Victorian shop and bar fronts. Locals flock to its autumn race meeting and harvest festival, while a more cosmopolitan crowd gathers for the annual **Listowel Writers' Week** *(see margin, right, and p.24–5)*.

Park in the town square. The **Tourist Information Office** is in **St John's Church**, the local arts centre. To explore the town, walk to the north side of the square and wander its few streets. Look out for **Allo's**, see ①③, on Church Street near the northeast corner of the square.

Listowel Castle

On the west side of the square is **Listowel Castle** (late May–mid-Sept daily 9.30am–5.30pm; guided tours only; charge), a 15th-century Fitz-maurice stronghold. Only part of its front survives, consisting of two large four-storey towers, rising to 15.3m (50ft), linked by an arch, and standing on a steep bank overlooking the River Feale. Go down the pedestrian way beside the castle, which leads to a pleasant green space beside the river, the best feature of Listowel.

Above from far left: Kerry County Museum; drama and races, Listowel.

Literary Listowel
Listowel is extremely proud of its literary heritage; local writers include John B. Keane *(The Field)* and Maurice Walsh *(The Quiet Man)*. Bigger international names feature during Listowel Writers' Week in early June.

Food and Drink

① DENNY LANE CAFÉ
Denny Lane, off Denny Street, Tralee; tel: 066-719 4319; B, L Mon–Sat, D Thur–Sat, June–Aug; €
This clean-lined contemporary café brings a touch of metro-politan chic to Tralee, serving excellent coffee, infusions and teas. The self-service counter has light dishes including chicken roulade or lasagne and salad. The homebaking, especially the scones, is outstanding.

② THE BUNKER
Cliff Road, Ballybunion; tel: 068-27934; B, L D daily; €
Perched midway between the Men's and Ladies' Strands, this large, bright yellow Victorian pub is hard to miss. Choose from a traditional menu with daily specials such as bacon and cabbage or roast leg of lamb, alongside home-made soup and toasted sandwiches. In summer the upstairs restaurant also serves dinner (€€).

③ ALLO'S BAR AND BISTRO
Church Street, Listowel; tel: 068-22880; B, L, D Tue–Sat; €
A traditional pub has been cleverly converted to a lively gastro-pub. Eat at the bar, or share an oil-cloth-covered table in the long narrow bar with the regulars. The salads are sensational, and local artisan foods are a feature of the extensive menu.

BUNRATTY, LIMERICK AND ADARE

Start learning about Ireland's past at Bunratty Castle and Folk Park. Then wander the medieval streets of Limerick, and discover its Georgian quarter, before driving south to explore the charming village of Adare.

Castle Country
During the 12th–15th centuries several monastic orders settled this area, while Irish clan chieftains built castles among the low hills and lakes to the northwest. The region is dotted with the ruins of fortified homes, some of which have been restored, the most magnificent being Bunratty Castle.

DISTANCE 35km (22 miles)

TIME A full day

START Bunratty

END Adare

POINTS TO NOTE

This tour is designed to start from Shannon Airport, but if you are travelling to Shannon from Kerry, start at Adare 17km (10 miles) southwest of Limerick on the N21. From Adare to Cork it is 92.5km (57½ miles) on the N21/N20.

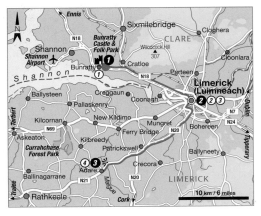

The Limerick region and the Shannon estuary have been of great strategic importance ever since the Vikings established a sheltered sea port on an island at the head of the Shannon estuary, now the city of Limerick.

BUNRATTY

Bunratty Castle ❶ (tel: 061-364 511; www.shannonheritage.com; daily 9am–5.30pm, last entry 4pm; charge) has a square tower at each corner and a drawbridge. Dating largely from the 16th century, it contains furniture and tapestries from the 14th to the 17th centuries. The extensive **Folk Park** (as above, last entry 4.15pm, June–Aug Sat–Sun until 6pm, last entry 5.15pm) has a number of reconstructed traditional dwellings, including a typical village street *c.*1880. Although **Durty Nelly's** pub (tel: 061-364 861) is on the riverbank beside the castle, it does not serve food in the daytime, so turn right out of the castle and soon you will see **J.P. Clarke's Country Pub**, see ⓸①.

Take the N18 south for some 14km (9 miles) to the city of Limerick.

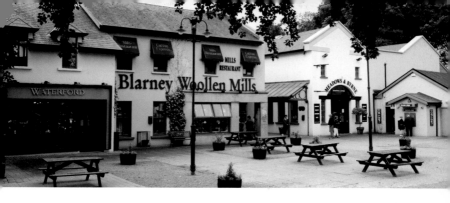

LIMERICK CITY

Founded by the Vikings in 812, Limerick takes its name from the Norse word, laemrich, meaning 'rich land'. Following the death of the King of Munster, the Normans captured Limerick in 1194, building city walls; shortly after, King John ordered an imposing fortification to be built on King's Island, now the historic centre. In the 18th century Limerick was extended further south with the construction of Newtown Pery, its Georgian quarter. The city went into decline after the founding of the Irish Free State in 1922, and suffered heavy emigration and much urban poverty. Its recovery began with the opening of Shannon Airport in 1947.

City Walk

The bulk of the low-lying city lies on the eastern bank of the River Shannon, and the wide, fast-flowing river is its best asset. Follow signs for the centre and **Arthur's Quay** car park; behind is the **Tourist Information Centre** (tel: 061-317 522; www.shannonregional tourism.ie; Mon–Sat 9am–6pm, July–Aug daily). Both the Shannon and, to the north, King John's Castle can be seen from here.

Hunt Museum

Turn right up Francis Street and left into Rutland Street for the **Hunt Museum** Ⓐ (tel: 061-312 833; www. huntmuseum.com; Mon–Sat 10am–5pm, Sun 2–5pm; charge). Once the city's Custom House, the compact Georgian building has the finest collection of Celtic and medieval treasures outside Dublin's National Museum, plus a small selection of Irish and European paintings, including works by Renoir and Picasso. Once a private collection, it was donated to the nation in 1976 by the Hunt family. There's also a shop and an excellent café.

St Mary's Cathedral

Turn left upon leaving the Hunt Museum and cross a bridge over a tributary of the Shannon to King's Island, site of the city's original settlement. On the left is **St Mary's Cathedral** Ⓑ (tel: 061-310 293; www.cathedral.limerick. anglican.org; daily 9am–5pm, Nov–Feb until 1pm; free). Much of the compact cruciform building dates from the 15th century, such as the black-oak misericords with carved animal features in the choir stalls. The rounded Romanesque entrance door is a remnant of the building's origins as a 12th-century palace belonging to Donal Mór O'Brien, King of Munster.

Above from far left: Bunratty Castle; crystal and woollen goods on sale at Bunratty Castle.

City of Youth
One reason why there are so many young people in Limerick is due to its university (www.ul.ie), a thriving institution founded in 1972 and currently with 11,000 students and 1,300 members of staff. Its campus at Plassey, 3km (2 miles) from the city centre off the N24 (Waterford road), is a showcase for modern architecture and design.

Food and Drink

① J.P. CLARKE'S COUNTRY PUB
Bunratty; tel: 061-363 363; daily L and D; €
Escape the tour-bus trade at this stylish modern pub close to the castle. The attractive high-ceilinged bar has an open fire and restaurant-style tables. The contemporary menu is strong on seafood; or try the beefburger with roast-pepper relish.

Above: altar and stained-glass detail, St Mary's, Limerick *(see p.81)*.

River Walk

In Adare you can go through the metal stile beside the Anglican church *(see opposite)* for a lovely rural riverside walk of about 1.5km (1 mile). The tour follows the banks of the River Maigue, rich in wildlife, to the west, before looping back to the village centre down Station Road.

King John's Castle

From the cathedral turn onto Nicholas Street and walk north for **King John's Castle** 🅒 (tel: 061-411 201; www.shannonheritage.com; daily 9.30am–5pm; charge), a massive fortification with curtain walls and two drum towers, built by the Normans in the 1200s and rebuilt and extended many times over the years. There are audio-visual displays which explain the castle's development, but the best part is the outdoor courtyard, which gives access to the massive bastions and great views of the river and city.

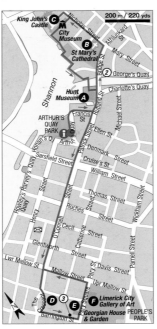

Riverside Footpath

Turn right out of the castle, and right again down a pedestrian alley beside the castle walls, past the **City Museum** (tel: 061-417 826; summer Mon–Sat 10am–5pm, Sun 2–5pm, winter Tue–Sat only; free), to return to the car park along a riverside footpath. At Merchant's Quay look for the modern footbridge across the river; alternatively, walk up to the road bridge to **The Locke Bar and Bistro**, see ⑪②.

Georgian Limerick

To extend your walk to Georgian Limerick, return to the Hunt Museum and walk south along Rutland Street and Patrick Street on to O'Connell Street. This is Limerick's main shopping area, and a brisk 20-minute walk will lead to the spacious streets of the Georgian area, which starts at the junction with Mallow Street.

The Crescent and Pery Square

The elegant four-storey houses in **The Crescent** 🅓 have been well restored. Turn left on to Barrington Street at the far end, and walk up to Pery Square. The corner house has been converted to a characterful hotel, a good spot for a break, see ⑪③. The house next door, **The Georgian House and Garden** 🅔 (2 Pery Square; tel: 061-314 130; Mon–Fri 10am–4.30pm; charge) dates from about 1830, and has been furnished appropriately to its period, with its original architectural features intact.

People's Park

On the opposite side of the road is the People's Park, one of Limerick's few green spaces, and the location of the **Limerick City Gallery of Art** ⑤ (Pery Square, tel: 061-310 633; Mon–Sat 10am–6pm, Sun 2–5pm; free), which has a permanent collection of Irish painting and contemporary shows. Walk to the corner with Mallow Street and turn left to rejoin O'Connell Street.

ADARE

Adare ③, which boasts of being 'Ireland's prettiest village', is only 17km (10 miles) southwest of Limerick on the N20, but it is in another world, so much so that it feels like walking on to a film set.

Heritage Centre and Priory

Adare is a tiny place, and you cannot miss the **Adare Heritage Centre** (Main Street; tel: 061-396 666; www. adareheritagecentre.ie; daily 9am–6pm; charge). There is a large car park here, plus several craft shops and a restaurant within. You can also pick up a map of the village here.

Turn left out of the Heritage Centre to the former **Trinitarian priory**, founded in 1230 and converted into a Catholic parish church in 1811. The opposite side of the wide main street is lined with thatched cottages. They were built in 1830 by the local landlord, the Earl of Dunraven, for his workers. Today, most of them are either restaurants or craft shops. Adare Cottage (tel: 061-396 422) is the most interesting of the latter, while the **Dunraven Arms**, see ⑪④, a traditional coaching inn now luxury hotel, is a good spot for breakfast or lunch.

Augustinian Friary

Turn left out of the Dunraven Arms, which marks the end of the village, and continue about 50m/yds to the former Augustinian friary, now Adare's **Anglican church**. To the north of the church are the well-preserved cloisters of the 1315 monastery. The church's nave and choir are also 14th century.

Above from far left: The Locke Bar and Bistro, Limerick; King John's Castle, Limerick; traditional ways of operating in Adare.

Luxury Lodgings
The main gates of Adare Manor (www. adaremanor.com) are across the road from the village's church. The manor, which was enlarged in the Tudor Revival style in the mid-19th century, is now a luxury hotel and golf resort.

Food and Drink

② THE LOCKE BAR AND BISTRO
3 George's Quay, Limerick; tel: 061-413 733; daily L and D; €
A traditional riverside pub with tables outside on the tree-lined quay, the Locke is a popular place for hearty pub grub and freshy made sandwiches. There's a quieter bar upstairs with table service.

③ ONE PERY SQUARE
1 Pery Square, Limerick; tel: 061-402 402; L, D €€
The elegant four-storey corner house has been converted into a stylish hotel, with unfussy decor mixing period and contemporary. The ground-floor lounge bar has lots of comfy sofas, and large windows, and a menu of soup, salads and superior sandwiches.

④ DUNRAVEN ARMS
Main Street, Adare; tel: 061-605 900; daily; B, L and D; €€
Now one of Ireland's leading hotels, the Dunraven Arms has not forgotten its origins as a village inn. Sample a coffee and scone or a light lunch in its traditional bar or bright, modern conservatory with a garden view.

DIRECTORY

A user-friendly alphabetical listing of practical information, plus hand-picked hotels and restaurants, clearly organised by area, to suit all budgets and tastes.

A–Z 86
ACCOMMODATION 96
RESTAURANTS 102

A

AGE RESTRICTIONS

The age of consent is 17. At 17 you can also apply for a driver's licence. The legal drinking age is 18, but some pubs will only serve those over 21 carrying photo ID. You must be 18 to buy cigarettes and tobacco. In the Republic of Ireland under 18s are not allowed on premises that serve alcohol after 9.30pm.

B

BUDGETING

The cost of a pint of draught beer starts from €3.80, and wine from about €4.50 for 175ml. Beer costs approximately €5 a pint in main Irish cities, and wine about €5.50 a glass, but it could be more in a fashionable bar and up to twice as much in a five-star hotel.

A main course at a budget restaurant costs €10–16, at a moderate one €18–26 and at an expensive one €27–36.

A double room with breakfast costs about €70–90 at a B&B or guesthouse, €90–140 at a moderate hotel and over €220 at an expensive hotel.

A single bus ticket in Cork or Limerick costs €1.60.

Admission to national museums is free. Charges for other heritage attractions vary from €3–12 and up.

A Heritage Card (adult: €21, family: €55) is excellent value, and gives free admission to about 20 sights and monuments in the southwest (www.heritageireland.ie). Heritage Island offers up to €500 worth of discounts at over 90 locations for two people travelling together, if you buy a copy of their guide (€6.99; www.heritage island.com).

C

CHILDREN

Irish people love children. They are usually welcome at hotels and B&Bs, most of which can offer cots or babysitting. Many hotels allow children to stay in their parents' room at no extra charge; check when booking. Some of the grander country houses will only accept children over 12.

Most restaurants can supply highchairs and a children's menu; bigger restaurants and pubs should have nappy-changing facilities. Kids are generally welcome in pubs up to about 7pm (and by law under 18s must be gone by 9.30pm), but this is at the discretion of the landlord, and children should be supervised by an adult at all times.

During holiday periods, there are plenty of child-oriented activities organised by museums, local festivals and outdoor centres; tourist offices *(see p.93)* will have full details.

CLOTHING

You can safely leave your formal clothes at home. Smart-casual is acceptable just about everywhere, and very few restaurants and hotels specify jacket and tie. Because of the unpredictability of the weather, pack an umbrella, some rainproof clothing and a warm sweater, even in summer. But bring the suncream as well; it does shine sometimes.

For climate information, see p.12.

CRIME AND SAFETY

While rural Ireland is a low-risk area for crime, hired cars are easy targets for criminals, and thefts from cars are commonplace in the cities of Cork and Limerick, and in the car parks of visitor attractions. Never leave anything visible in your car, even if you are only leaving it briefly. Be careful when withdrawing money from ATMs, and shield your PIN. Beware of pickpockets in crowded places. It is sensible to keep a copy of your passport in case of theft.

Victims of crime in the Republic should contact Irish Tourist Assistance Service, Garda HQ, Harcourt Street, Dublin 2; tel: 01-478 5295 (helpline tel: 1890-365 700); www.itas.ie.

For emergencies, see p.88.

CUSTOMS

Visitors of all nationalities entering or leaving the EU via Ireland must declare on arrival or departure sums of cash above €10,000.

Visitors within the EU may import the following goods, provided they were purchased within the EU and are for personal use: 800 cigarettes, 400 cigarillos, 200 cigars, 1kg tobacco, 10 litres spirits, 20 litres fortified wines, 90 litres wine, 110 litres beer.

From outside the EU you may import duty-free: 200 cigarettes or the tobacco equivalent, 4 litres of wine or 1 litre of spirits, and other goods to the value of €430 per person.

For details of restricted goods, see www.revenue.ie.

Non-EU visitors can claim back sales taxes on purchases made in the Republic. Participating stores have a 'Tax Free Shopping' sign in the window. You must complete a tax refund document, and present this and the goods to customs on departure. Some airports will refund you on the spot; otherwise, mail the validated document back to the store, and a refund will be issued. The VAT rate on most items is 21 percent.

D

DISABLED TRAVELLERS

Ireland is still introducing facilities such as ramps and accessible toilets for people with disabilities. Public transport lags behind, especially outside Dublin. However, visitors often find

Above from far left: city flag; enjoying a siesta in Enniskerry.

that people's helpfulness makes up for the lack of amenities.

In the Republic, the key organisation for practical information, wheelchair rental and parking permits is the Irish Wheelchair Association (Áras Chúchulainn, Blackheath Drive, Clontarf, Dublin; tel: 01-818 6400; www.iwa.ie). The official government body is the National Disability Authority (25 Clyde Road, Ballsbridge, Dublin 4; tel: 01-608 0400; www.nda.ie). The Head Office of Fáilte Ireland *(see p.93)* can advise on attractions and accommodation suitable for disabled visitors.

E

ELECTRICITY

The standard is 220 volts AC (50 cycles). Hotels usually have dual 220/110 voltage sockets for electric razors.

Most sockets require a 3-pin plug; visitors may need an adaptor.

EMBASSIES AND CONSULATES

Dublin

Australia: Fitzwilton House, Wilton Terrace, Dublin 2; tel: 01-664 5300; www.ireland.embassy.gov.au.
Britain: 29 Ballsbridge Terrace, Dublin 4; tel: 01-205 3700; www. britishembassyinireland.fco.gov.uk.
Canada: 7–8 Wilton Terrace, Dublin 2; tel: 01-234 4000; www.canada.ie.

US: 42 Elgin Road, Dublin 4; tel: 01-668 8777; http://dublin.usembassy.gov.

Belfast

American Consulate General. Danesfort House, 223 Stranmillis Road, Belfast BT9 5GR; tel: 028-9038 6100; www.usembassy.org.uk/nireland.

EMERGENCIES

In an emergency, dial 999; 112 is also used in the Republic.

ETIQUETTE

The Irish generally live up to their reputation of loving to talk, and they expect visitors to respond in kind. Do not wait to be introduced; strike up a conversation with the person sitting next to you at the bar or on the bus, and be prepared to tell your life story. In Ireland it is perfectly acceptable to talk to strangers; no one will think you are crazy for this.

Pub etiquette is based on good manners: if somebody buys you a drink, buy one back; if a group includes you in the drinks order (a 'round'), offer to buy the next one. It's good practice to avoid being drawn into discussions of politics or religion while alcohol is being consumed. You should also avoid telling people what's wrong with their country (eg the roads, the signposts, the high cost of everything); they know already.

G

GAY/LESBIAN ISSUES

There should be no major problems for gay and lesbian travellers in southwest Ireland. Be as safety-conscious as you would in any city or country. Openly gay couples may attract unwanted attention in small-town pubs.

Information on bars and clubs, accommodation and friendly contacts can be found on www.queer.ie. The following offers advice and contacts:

Cork: The Other Place, St Augustine Street; tel: 021-427 8470; www.theotherplaceclub.ie.

GREEN ISSUES

Ireland has an active Green Party, but green issues and sustainable planning are minority concerns. Recycling is in its infancy, and much waste still goes to landfill; however, a small charge for plastic bags in supermarkets has been effective. Solar and wind energy are gaining in popularity, although there is some resistance to wind farms. Many of Ireland's smaller farms are now managed under the Rural Environment Protection Scheme, to encourage wildlife and biological diversity. But overuse of fertiliser in farming and forestry has led to pollution of lakes and rivers. For the latest, visit http://friendsoftheirishenvironment.net. For carbon-offsetting your trip, *see above right*.

Carbon-Offsetting

Air travel produces a huge amount of carbon dioxide and is a significant contributor to global warming. If you would like to offset the damage caused to the environment by your flight, a number of organisations can do this for you using online 'carbon calculators' that tell you how much you need to donate. In the UK travellers can visit www.jpmorganclimatecare.com or www.carbonneutral.com; in the US log on to https://climatefriendly.com or www.sustainabletravelinternational.org.

H

HEALTH

Medical insurance is advisable for all visitors. However, visitors from EU countries are entitled to medical treatment in the Republic of Ireland under reciprocal arrangements.

With the exception of UK citizens, visitors from EU states should obtain the European Health Insurance Card, which entitles the holder to free treatment by a doctor and free medicines on prescription. If hospital treatment is necessary, this will be given free in a public ward. UK visitors need only go to a doctor (or, in an emergency, a hospital), present some proof of identity (eg a driving licence) and request treatment under the EU health agreement.

Above from far left: a nation of animal-lovers; at Listowel Writers' Festival; be prepared for wet weather.

Hospitals and Pharmacies

Cork: Cork University Hospital, Wilton, Cork; tel: 021-454 6400; www.cuh.hse.ie

Phelan's Midnight Pharmacy, Kinsale Road Roundabout, Cork; tel: 021-431 0132

Limerick: Midwestern Regional Hospital, Dooradoyle, Limerick; tel: 061-482 219; www.3bv.org

Arthur's Quay Pharmacy, 17 The Crescent, Limerick, Co. Limerick; tel: 042-969 0099

Tralee: Tralee General Hospital, Rathass, Tralee, Co. Kerry; tel: 066-712 6222

Ashe Street Pharmacy, 10 Ashe Street, Tralee, Co. Kerry; tel: 066-719 0931

HOURS AND HOLIDAYS

Shops and department stores usually open Mon–Sat 9.30am–5.30 or 6pm. In smaller towns some shops close for lunch between 1pm and 2pm. Supermarkets and convenience stores generally open daily until 9pm. Post offices open Mon–Fri 9am–5.30pm and Sat 9am–1pm. Government offices are open Mon–Fri 9am–5pm.

Museums and other tourist sights are often closed on Monday, and most have restricted opening hours between November and Easter or late May.

In hotels and B&Bs, breakfast is generally served from 8–10am, and in restaurants and pubs until noon. Restaurants and pubs generally serve lunch between 12.30 and 2.30pm, and dinner from 6 to 9.30pm.

Public Holidays

1 Jan: New Year's Day
17 Mar: St Patrick's Day
Mar/Apr: Good Fri and Easter Mon
1st Mon May: May Day
Last Mon May: Bank Holiday (NI*)
1st Mon June: Bank Holiday (RoI**)
12 July: Bank Holiday (NI)
1st Mon Aug: Bank Holiday (RoI)
Last Mon Aug: Bank Holiday (NI)
Last Mon Oct: Bank Holiday (RoI)
25 Dec: Christmas Day
26 Dec: Boxing Day
* NI = Northern Ireland
** RoI - Republic of Ireland

I

INTERNET FACILITIES

Wi-fi is widely available free in cafés, bars and public areas of hotels. Most hotels also have a computer available for public access.

MAPS

Cyclists and walkers may want large-scale maps; these can be bought locally from bookshops, newsagents and tourist information offices. Tourist offices usually also offer free maps of the town and surrounding area.

Above from far left: making traditional music; where to go for your very own fiddle or bodhran.

MEDIA

Print Media. The *Irish Times* is Ireland's newspaper of record, with good coverage of foreign news, arts and business. The *Irish Independent* is published daily in Dublin, and the *Irish Examiner* in Cork. The *Examiner* is widely read throughout the region. It also publishes *The Echo*, an evening paper with Cork and Limerick editions, useful for entertainment listings.

Television and Radio. In the Republic RTÉ (www.rte.ie) broadcasts three channels including the Irish-language TG4 (www.tg4.ie). Most UK channels are available on satellite or cable, which is widespread in hotels and B&Bs (confirm on booking). RTÉ1 is the main radio station for news, current affairs and drama, 2FM plays pop music, and Lyric FM is for lovers of classical music. There are also a number of independent local radio stations.

MONEY

Currency. The Republic of Ireland is in the Eurozone. Banknotes come in denominations of €5, €10, €20, €50, €100, €200 and €500; coins in denominations of 1, 2, 5, 10, 20 and 50 cents, plus €1 and €2.

Banking Hours. Banks are open Mon–Fri 10am–4pm, with one day late opening until 5pm (Thur in Cork). Smaller town banks may close for lunch from 12.30–1.30pm.

Cash Machines. Nearly all banks have 24-hour cash machines (ATMs), but not all towns have banks. In smaller places, cash machines can be found in convenience stores. Check with your bank before leaving home to confirm that your bankcard will work in Ireland.

Credit Cards. The most widely accepted cards are Visa and Mastercard, followed by American Express. Many, but not all guesthouses and B&Bs, take credit cards; check in advance of your stay.

Tipping. This is not expected in bars, except in lounge bars where drinks are brought to your table. It is usual to give at least a 10 percent tip to waiting staff. Round-up taxi fares to the nearest euro or pound, and porters are usually given about €1 a bag.

P

POLICE

The Republic is policed by the Garda Síochána (Guardians of the Peace). In an emergency, dial 999 or 112.

POST

Postage stamps are sold by post offices, newsagents and general stores. Letters and postcards cost 55 cents to send within the Republic and 82 cents to the UK, mainland Europe and North America. In the Republic most letter

boxes are pillar-box-shaped and are painted green.

Post Offices. Hours are generally Mon–Fri 9am–5.30pm and Sat 9am–1pm.

R

RELIGION

The free practice of religion is guaranteed by the constitution in the Republic, and there is no state religion. However, most of the population is Catholic. The second-largest congregation is the Episcopalian-affiliated Church of Ireland. Church attendance on Sundays by Catholics remains a strong tradition in southwest Ireland.

S

SMOKING

Smoking is banned in all workplaces, including taxis, bars, restaurants and nightclubs. A few hotels have bedrooms in which smoking is permitted: ask when booking. Elaborate sheltered outdoor smoking areas are provided by many pubs and clubs.

T

TELEPHONES

The international dialling code for the Republic of Ireland is 353. There are several telecommunications companies operating in Ireland, the largest one being Eircom (www.eircom.ie). Public telephones mainly use phonecards, which are widely available from newsagents and supermarkets. Phone boxes are gradually disappearing, as the mobile (cell) phone gains dominance.

International calls can be dialled direct from private phones, or dial 114 for the international operator. To contact the local operator, dial 10. The long-distance services of BT Ireland, AT&T, Sprint and MCI are also available.

Mobile (Cell) Phones. Only mobiles with GSM will work in Ireland. If your phone is non-GSM, consult with your provider before travelling. It may be cheaper to buy a local SIM card and top up with prepaid calls. Local providers include 3, Meteor, 02, Tescomobile and Vodafone. If you are coming from the UK, you will need international roaming in the Republic.

TIME ZONES

Ireland follows Greenwich Mean Time. In spring, the clock moves one hour ahead for Summer Time; in autumn it moves back to GMT. At noon – according to GMT – it is 4am in Los Angeles, 7am in New York, 1pm in Western Europe, 8pm in Singapore, 10pm in Sydney and midnight in New Zealand.

TOILETS

Public toilets are usually available in a town's main car park, at tourist offices and at big petrol stations. Most large supermarkets and all department stores have public toilets. Most pubs reserve their toilets for their customers' use only.

TOURIST INFORMATION

Fáilte Ireland. The Irish tourist board. Tel: 0808-234 2009. See www.discover ireland.com for full details.

Regional Offices. A number are mentioned in the tours in this guide; otherwise, see www.discoverireland.ie.

TRANSPORT

Arrival by Air

There are flights from Britain and Europe to Cork and Shannon airports, with more than 30 airlines flying from 70 destinations. There are also frequent flights from British airports to Kerry Airport at Farranfore, which is midway between Killarney and Tralee. Internal flights operate from Dublin to Cork, Kerry and Shannon airports.

The main carriers from Britain are Aer Arran (www.aerarran.com), Aer Lingus (www.aerlingus.com) and Ryanair (www.ryanair.com).

There are direct flights from the US to Shannon Airport. The main carriers are Aer Lingus (www.aerlingus.com), Continental Airlines (www.continental.com), Delta Airlines (www.delta.com) and US Airways (www.usairways.com).

To/From Cork Airport

The bus from Cork Airport (tel: 021-431 3131; www.corkairport.com) to the city takes about 10 minutes. A taxi from Cork Airport to the city centre (8km/5miles) costs from €10–15. Skylink and Bus Éireann run bus services to the city centre for about €4 single. From Shannon Airport (tel: 061-471 444; www.shannonairport.com) there is a regular bus service to Limerick city (30 min). Kerry International Airport (tel: 066-976 4644) is on the Bus Éireann network, and has services to Tralee, Killarney and Limerick. See www.buseireann.ie for timetables.

A taxi from the airport to the city centre should cost approximately €10–15 in Cork and €35 in Shannon (to Limerick).

For more information on access to and from airports, see www.discover ireland.com.

Arrival by Sea

To travel to the southwest from the UK, the most convenient ports of arrival are Rosslare (Co. Wexford) or Cork. There is a direct service from Roscoff to Cork. For details of operators and routes, see www.discover ireland.com.

Above from far left: Irish post boxes are an eye-catching green; at Cahirmee Horse Fair; painted wheel.

Public Transport in Ireland

The bus network is more extensive and more flexible than the train. Bus Éireann (tel: 01-836 6111; www.bus eireann.ie) has both local and direct express services. Its Expressway timetable (€3) is essential if you plan to travel by bus, and its Open Road passes allow flexible cross-country travel. The main bus stations in the southwest are at Cork (Parnell Place; tel: 021-450 8188), Tralee (Casement Railway Station; tel: 066-716 4700) and Limerick (Colbert Railway Station; tel: 061-313 333).

Iarnród Éireann (Irish Rail; tel: 01-836 6222; www.irishrail.ie) runs rail services from Dublin to Limerick, Cork, Killarney and Tralee. The Cork line terminates at Cork; to travel from Cork to destinations on the Tralee line you must backtrack to the junction at Mallow. There is also a suburban commuter line from Cork to Cobh and to Midleton.

Fares are generally reasonable (eg Dublin–Cork return: €55, or €20 each way booked online). Visitors aged 66 and over are entitled to free rail travel: register online for your Golden Trekker pass at least 48 hours before arrival at www.discoverireland. com or contact Tourism Ireland on tel: 0800-039 7000. Ireland is one of 21 countries in which you can use the global or one-country Eurailpass (www.eurail.com). Irish Rail also has special-value tickets for visitors.

Taxis

There are metered taxis in Cork, Killarney, Tralee and Limerick. To avoid problems, in other areas, fares should be agreed beforehand. Cork Taxi Co-op, 6 Washington Street, Cork, tel: 021-427 2222, is one of the biggest companies in Cork.

Driving

Outside the cities, Irish roads are still among the least congested in Europe, although it is hard to believe this when you are stuck in a traffic jam on the ring roads of Cork or Killarney, or in the notoriously clogged-up centre of Tralee. Most national and regional routes, including the Ring of Kerry, consist of two-lane roads, with limited opportunities for overtaking.

It is traditional for slow-moving traffic to pull over on to the hard shoulder when there is one, and let the tail of cars behind pass. The southwest has some of the narrowest, most winding roads in the country, many of them in mountainous regions. These are pointed out, where applicable, in the relevant tour.

Rules of the Road. Drive on the left. All passengers must wear seat belts. Drink-driving laws are strict, and it is an offence to drive with a concentration of alcohol exceeding 80mg per 100ml of blood.

Remember that speed-limit signs are in kilometres. The limit is 45kmh (28mph) in urban areas,

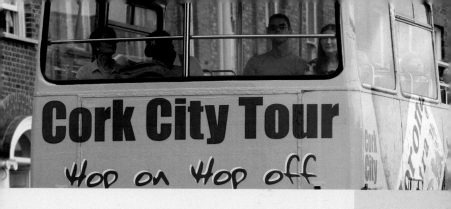

80kmh (50mph) on non-national roads, 100kmh (62mph) on national routes (green signposts) and 120kmh (75mph) on motorways. Note that on-the-spot fines can be issued for speeding offences.

Tolls. There is a toll charge of €1.90 for using the M8 Fermoy bypass.

Language. By law signposts to destinations in Irish-speaking areas must be in Irish only. The most important one to note is An Daingean, which is Irish for Dingle. The town will be marked as Dingle on your map, but the only signposts you will see will read 'An Daingean'.

Car Hire. Be sure to book in advance for July and August. Car hire is expensive in Ireland, and advance booking as part of a fly-drive or train-ferry-drive package often leads to a better deal, as does booking online. Drivers under 25 and over 70 may have to pay a higher rate. Most companies will not rent cars to people over 76. The big international car-hire companies have offices in all major cities, airports and ferry terminals.

Local and international car-hire companies are listed on www.carhireireland.com.

V

VISAS AND PASSPORTS

UK citizens do not require a passport to enter Ireland, but most carriers by air or sea ask for a photographic ID, in practice usually either a passport or driving licence. Check with the individual company you are travelling with before leaving.

Non-UK nationals must have a valid passport. EU nationals and travellers from the US, Canada, Australia, New Zealand and South Africa are simply required to show a valid passport. Visitors of all other nationalities should get in contact with their local Irish embassy or consulate for up-to-date information before travelling.

W

WEBSITES

• www.discoverireland.com (the official website of Fáilte Ireland)
• www.entertainment.ie (for theatre, cinema, club and festival listings)
• www.gulliver.ie (accommodation reservation network of Fáilte Ireland)
• www.hostels-ireland.com (Tourist Board-approved holiday hostels)
• www.met.ie (for weather forecasts)

WEIGHTS AND MEASURES

The metric system has been adopted in Ireland, but is not always enforced, and a mixture of units is still used in day-to-day life. For example, beer comes in pints, petrol comes in litres, while food is sold in both pounds and in kilograms.

Above from far left: bright taxi lights; a Cork City Tour bus, with hop-on, hop-off options, can be a good way to see the sights.

While the southwest has some luxurious country-house hotels, even the most expensive places are pleasantly informal. The middle-range includes new hotels with good facilities, and converted period buildings. The inexpensive hotels tend to be family-owned establishments, or guesthouses. Outside Cork and Limerick, many businesses close between November and mid-March.

Book in advance in July and August, especially in west Cork, the Ring of Kerry and Dingle, and on Bank Holiday weekends *(see p.90)*. At other times of the year ask for a reduced rate if you are staying more than one night, and check out hotel websites for special deals. For self-catering options, see www.discover ireland.com.

Cork City

Ambassador Hotel

Military Hill, St Lukes; tel: 021-455 1996; www.ambassadorhotelcork.ie; €€

St Lukes is Cork's boho quarter, and the Ambassador a much-loved land-mark. Its ornate red-brick façade dates from 1870, and the hotel has splendid views of the docks and the River Lee. The Victorian-style bar and restaurant are popular with locals, while the bedrooms are unusually spacious with high ceilings, and classic decor. It's in a quiet inner suburb, only a short down-hill walk to the city centre.

Gabriel House

Summerhill North, St Luke's Cross; tel: 021-450 0333; www.gabriel housecork.com; €

This large detached building was previously a Christian Brothers seminary, but makes a characterful budget hotel. It's on a bluff high above the railway station, a five-minute uphill walk from the centre, and also has free car parking. The best and largest rooms have a river view, and there's an all-day cafeteria.

Hayfield Manor

Perrott Avenue, College Road; tel: 021-484 5900; www.hayfieldmanor. ie; €€€€€

Tucked away in a quiet side street near the university, this Georgian-style manor house is surrounded by quiet gardens, and is more like a rural retreat than a city hotel. With two restaurants and the Manor Bar, the place buzzes with beautiful people. The luxurious bedrooms are individually designed in the Victorian style, and the spa is exclusive to residents.

Price for a double room for one night with breakfast	
€€€€€	over 220 euros
€€€€	160–220 euros
€€€	120–160 euros
€€	90–120 euros
€	under 90 euros

East Cork

Ballymakeigh House

Killeagh; tel: 024-95184; http://home
page.eircom.net/~ballymakeigh
house; €

Margaret Browne's farmhouse B&B,
located midway between Shanagarry
and the sandy beaches of Youghal,
is renowned. From the conservatory
behind the house you can view the
herd of dairy cows, while sampling a
home-made strawberry muffin, part
of an exceptional breakfast. Rooms
are hotel-standard, and the welcome
is warm and effusive.

Gilbert's Restaurant and Townhouse

Pearse Square, Cobh; tel: 021-481
1300; www.gilbertsincobh.com; €

A solid Victorian building with a
fine limestone façade in Cobh's central square, just below the cathedral,
has been converted into a bistro
with rooms overhead. The rooms are
attractively designed, with a spare,
continental chic, including wooden
floors, louvred shutters and contemporary paintings.

Blarney Castle and the Lee Valley

Seaview House Hotel

Ballylickey, Bantry; tel; 027-50073;
www.seaviewhousehotel.com; €€€

This country house is set in its own
wooded grounds on the shores of
Bantry Bay. Owner-manager Kathleen

O'Sullivan has created a pleasantly
old-fashioned hotel out of what was
once her home. The bedrooms are
individually decorated with genuine
antiques, and have views over the
sheltered waters of inner Bantry Bay,
and the mountains beyond. There is an
excellent restaurant and a quiet bar.

The White House

Shean Lower, Blarney; tel: 021-438
5338; www.thewhitehouseblarney.
com; €

You can see Blarney Castle from the
front door of this modest B&B, a
bungalow set a height above the road
to the village, within walking distance
of all amenities. Hosts Pat and Regina
Coughlan both have a professional
background in the hotel business, and
standards are exceptionally high: all is
sparkling clean, warm and comfortable.
Home baking features on the breakfast menu, and your hosts can provide
knowledgeable touring advice.

The Blackwater Valley and North Cork

Ballyvolane House

Castlelyons, near Fermoy, Co. Cork;
tel: 025-36349; www.ballyvolane
house.ie; €€€€

This is a genuine Irish country house.
Originally built in 1728, Ballyvolane
was enlarged in the 19th century,
and is now an imposing two-storey
mansion set amid idyllic gardens.
Fly-fishing on the Blackwater is a

**Above from far
left:** Hayfield Manor
(interior and exte-
rior) is a luxurious
retreat in Cork city.

major attraction, and there is a lively calendar of events including canoeing and walking weekends. The bedrooms are large and wittily decorated with antiques and heirlooms. Meet the other guests over dinner, served at the family dining table.

Richmond House

Cappoquin, Co. Waterford; tel; 058-54278; www.richmondhouse.net; €€€

This is a small country-house hotel, with only nine rooms, set in its own grounds in the neighbouring village to Lismore, owned and run by a talented chef, Paul Deevey, and his wife, Claire, and an extremely friendly staff. It's a haven of peace, scented by the log fires burning in the elegantly proportioned drawing room, and the restaurant to which it leads. The restaurant is very popular with non-residents, which creates a nice evening buzz. The rooms are various shapes and sizes, all individually decorated, with lovely views.

Kinsale to Roaringwater Bay

The Glen Country House

Kilbrittain; tel: 023-884 9862; www.glencountryhouse.com; €€

The creeper-clad Victorian house, deep in the Cork countryside, is a decidedly up-market version of the average Irish farmhouse, furnished with beautiful antiques and striking contemporary paintings by the owner's uncle, the

Irish artist, Patrick Scott. The family gives its guests the run of the house, and many return time and again. Bedrooms are spacious, attractively decorated and impeccably maintained, with distant sea views. There are two good restaurants nearby.

Heron's Cove

The Harbour, Goleen, near Schull; tel: 028-35225; www.heronscove.com; €

Heron's Cove, just off the main road (R591), is an incredibly peaceful spot. The house is modern and very comfortable, perched right on the water's edge of a quiet harbour. The rooms are simple and unfussy, with plain coral-coloured walls and carpets, and have picture windows overlooking the water. To top it all, on the ground floor there is an excellent seafood restaurant run by the owner's son.

Trident Hotel

Pier Head, Kinsale; tel: 021-477 2301; www.tridenthotel.com; €€

A modern hotel, with much plate glass, the Trident is built around three side of a former boat-building yard adjacent to the town's main pier. The fourth side is the sea. All bedrooms have sea views, and breakfast is taken in a first-floor room with panoramic harbour views. Large container ships sometimes dock outside, blocking part of the view, but this only adds to the charm.

Bantry Bay

Blair's Cove House

Durrus; tel: 027-61127; www.blairs
cove.ie; €€€€

This gorgeous Georgian country
house at the top of Dunmanus Bay
is painted blue. The house is built
around a courtyard, and there is also
self-catering accommodation, and
cobbled paths on which to explore
the beautiful gardens. The Courtyard
restaurant, with its open wood-fired
grill, is an added bonus.

Hillcrest House

Ahakista; tel: 027-67045; email:
hillcrestfarm@ahakista.com; €

A traditional farmhouse on a hill
overlooking Dunmanus Bay. Joe and
Agnes Hegarty will greet you with
home-baked scones and a pot of tea.
Three downstairs rooms have patios
with outdoor tables, while the upstairs
rooms have traditional hipped ceilings.
The 'playroom' with table tennis and
darts for rainy days is a nice touch.

The Maritime Hotel

The Quay, Bantry; tel: 027-54700;
www.themaritime.ie; €€€€

This is a 117-room modern hotel on
the water's edge, built on a long narrow
site, so that all rooms have a sea view.
Rooms are spacious, with floor-to-
ceiling windows, extra-large beds,
flat-screen TVs and large bathrooms.
The leisure centre has an indoor pool,
and the bar is buzzing day and night.

Ring of Beara

Dzogchen Beara Retreat Centre

Garranes, Allihies; tel: 027-73032;
www.dzogchenbeara.org; €

Midway between Castletownbere and
Allihies, on a remote cliff top with
uninterrupted views of the Atlantic,
many people choose to stay in dormi-
tory accommodation at the Buddhists'
farmhouse hostel, or to rent a self-
catering cottage simply to enjoy the
peace and beauty of the surroundings.

Sallyport House

Glengarriff Road, Kenmare,
Co. Kerry; tel: 064-664 2066;
www.sallyporthouse.com; €€

Just outside Kenmare, near the Beara
road, this solidly built family home on
the bank of the Kenmare River has
been converted into a comfortable
B&B. The bedrooms all have harbour
or mountain views and are furnished
with antiques that have been in the
family for generations. There is an
interesting breakfast menu served in a
sunny room overlooking the garden.

Killarney

Friar's Glen

Mangerton Road, Muckross; tel:
064-663 7500; www.friarsglen.ie; €

This stone-fronted house was pur-
pose-built as a B&B in a traditional
style. It is set in 11 hectares (28 acres)
of National Park (about 3km/2 miles
outside town near Muckross Park),

Above from far
left: garden at
Richmond House;
terrace at the
Trident Hotel;
indoor pool at the
Maritime Hotel.

and deer sometimes venture into the garden in the early morning. Inside, a baronial pine staircase leads to spacious, well-appointed bedrooms with mahogany furniture, and lovely views.

The Malton
Town Centre; tel: 064-663 8000; www.themalton.com; €€€

This hotel opened in 1854, just across from the station, to coincide with the arrival of the railway in Killarney. It is grandiose, with a pillared entrance portico leading to imposing public rooms with high-domed ceilings and large windows. Nowadays it's a lively spot, with the bistro-style Peppers restaurant and a popular bar creating a good buzz. The comfortable bedrooms are bigger in the main house than those in the newer 'garden wing'.

The Ring of Kerry
Atlantic Villa
Knightstown, Valentia Island; tel: 066-947 6839; www.anirish experience.com; €

This compact black-and-white Victorian villa has sea views to the north and garden views to the south. All rooms are individually decorated, comfortable and characterful. Hosts Brian and Jackie Morgan are welcoming and helpful, and Brian is an ace cook. Guests share the one dining table at breakfast. Evening meals can be pre-booked off season, and the pub is just around the corner.

Brook Lane Hotel
Kenmare; tel: 064-42077; www.brooklanehotel.com; €€

A quiet location on the edge of the village is a plus at this relatively new hotel, constructed in the traditional style with steep gables and stone-fronted wings. It offers great value for money, with comfortable, well-appointed rooms, leather armchairs and open fires in the lounge, and a choice of restaurants.

Parknasilla Resort
Sneem; tel: 064-667 5600; www.parknasillahotel.ie; €€€€€

Located on a sheltered sea inlet, far from any other building, this large Victorian hotel has had many famous guests. It's been discreetly modernised and has a great pool and spa, as well as self-catering houses to help the budget. There are many kilometres of walks within the grounds, and it is very peaceful.

The Dingle Peninsula
Dingle Skellig & Peninsula Spa
Dingle; tel: 066-915 0200; www.dingleskellig.com; €€€€

The only place in town with an indoor pool, the Skellig is equally popular with Irish families and weekending couples. Built on the water's edge at the entrance to town, it has one of the few restaurants in town with a sea view, and a gorgeously sited open-air hot tub. The bar is a lively spot.

Greenmount House
Upper John Street, Dingle; tel:
066-915 1414; www.greenmount
house.ie; €€
Only a short walk from the town
centre, this quiet 14-room guesthouse is surrounded by fields and has
a lovely view of the sun setting over
Dingle Harbour. Rooms are spacious,
with uncluttered contemporary decor,
wooden floors, plump sofas and extra-
large beds. The home baking and
breakfast here are renowned.

Tralee and North Kerry
Brook Manor Lodge
Fenit Road; tel: 066-712 0406;
www.brookmanorlodge.com; €
Follow the signposts for Fenit from
Tralee to find this 8-room country
B&B, a large pink house 2km (1 mile)
from the town. It makes an excellent
touring base, with a large, comfortably
furnished room to come back to at the
end of the day, and an excellent breakfast served in the conservatory.

The Grand Hotel
Denny Street, Tralee; tel: 066-712
1499; www.grandhoteltralee.com;
€€
Three large Georgian houses in the
centre of Tralee make up the Grand
Hotel. There is a great sense of tradition in the bar and lobby, with carved
mantelpieces and Victorian spoonback
chairs. Bedrooms are a bit small, due
to the age of the building, but well

equipped and great value. Food is
cooked to order at breakfast, and the
service is attentive.

Adare, Limerick and Shannon
Carrygerry Country House
Newmarket-on-Fergus, Co. Clare;
tel: 061-360 500; www.carrygerry
house.com; €€€
A quirky detached house dating from
1793, way out in the country, with
long views to the Shannon estuary.
Carrygerry is only 8km (5 miles)
from Shannon Airport and so very
convenient. Owner-chef Niall Ennis
oversees the excellent Conservatory
Restaurant, while his wife Gillian
supervises the 11 guest rooms, which
are furnished with modest antiques.
Pay attention to the directions on the
website before setting out.

Patrick Punch's Hotel
Punch's Cross, Limerick; tel: 061-
460 800; www.dghotels.com; €–€€
One of the better results of the boom
years is the expansion of a traditional
crossroads pub into a funky, 72-room
hotel with 15m (50ft) pool in its
well-equipped fitness club. The vast
reception area has floor-to-ceiling
glass, and red leather armchairs, and
the bedrooms are large and airy. The
original pub is still there, along with
a swanky restaurant, Dish. Rates vary
with demand – you could bag yourself
a bargain.

Above from far
left: room *(far left)*,
exterior *(centre)* and
pool *(above)* at the
Parknasilla Resort.

After years in the gastronomic wilderness, the southwest has become one of the most food-conscious areas in Ireland *(see p.14)*. Chefs and producers here are proud to be leading the way in the revival of traditional skills, and in innovative cooking.

Some of the best up-market restaurants are in hotels, but now they are more likely to offer *sushi* or *confit* of duck than the overcooked meat and soggy vegetables of yesteryear. The dining scene is consistently informal; even the grandest venues specify 'smart but casual': a jacket for men, but no obligatory tie.

In the middle price range, especially in pub restaurants, the emphasis is still on hearty fare: large portions of meat and fish, and lots of potatoes; vegetables might still be a bit of a rarity. Nearly all restaurants are fighting the recession with cut-price menus of all kinds, some based on the day's market, others confined to certain hours.

The best value is bar food, served at lunch time and early evening. At weekends, and in July and August, booking is advisable.

Cork City

Café Paradiso
16 Lancaster Quay, Western Road, Cork; tel: 021-427 4973; www.cafe paradiso.ie; Tue–Sat L, D; €–€€€
Inspired chef and cookery writer Denis Cotter creates vegetarian dishes that never fail to excite the palate, so that even carnivores relish every mouthful. The pumpkin risotto is renowned, as are his roast aubergine parcels of spinach, walnut and Coolea cheese with cherry tomato and caper sauce. The service is friendly and efficient in spite of the rather cramped, ever-busy space, usually packed with people from the nearby university. Buy one of Cotter's books for insight into his thinking.

Greenes
48 MacCurtain Street, Cork; tel: 021-450 0011; daily D, Sun L; €€€
Turn off the busy street into a cobblestoned alley for a pleasant surprise: at night it is floodlit, and a natural waterfall runs down one wall, while by day there are outdoor tables. Part of a Victorian warehouse conversion, the restaurant has a minimalist modern interior with exposed stone walls, and features stylish green rattan chairs. Seafood is the speciality on the French chef's menu (try his *bouillabaisse* of the day), but meat dishes and vegetarian food are also offered, usually in the guise of classic French creations.

Cork Harbour and East Cork

Gilbert's Restaurant
11 Pearse Square, Cobh; tel: 021-481 1300; B, L, D daily; €–€€
The ground floor of a substantial Victorian house in Cobh's central square has been stripped out and reincarnated

Above from
far left: Café
Paradiso; French-
style desserts.

as a snazzy brasserie. The original parquet floor is complemented by uncluttered modern decor, wooden-top tables, and plain white crockery. Try a 'Gilbert's Special' for breakfast (egg baked with cream and Serrano ham), a light lunch, or your choice from the extensive à la carte dinner menu of locally sourced produce, including rib-eye steak and rack of lamb.

Blarney and the Lee Valley

Blairs Inn

Cloghroe, Blarney, Co. Cork; tel: 021-438 1470; www.blairsinn.ie; daily L, D; €€

This traditional riverside country pub five minutes' drive from the castle (follow signs for Cloghroe off the R617) is the perfect antidote to the tourist crowds at Blarney. The white-washed walls are famous for their hanging baskets in summer, and you can eat outdoors beneath an awning. There is a welcoming traditional dark-wood interior with open fires in winter. Blairs Inn is known for sound cooking and a range of fairly traditional meat, seafood dishes, vegetarian options and game in season.

Blackwater Valley

Eamonn's Place

Main Street, Lismore; tel: 058-54025; Mon–Fri L, June–Sept L and D; €

Like many rural pubs, Eamonn's Place, a traditional hostelry in the centre of Lismore, has had to diversify to survive. The front bar is a traditional pint-drinkers' haunt, while simple, freshly prepared food – soup, sandwiches and hot dishes of the day – is served in a separate restaurant area that leads on to a stone-walled town garden.

The President's Restaurant

Longueville House, Mallow; tel: 022-47156; www.longuevillehouse.ie; closed Jan–mid-Mar, D; €€€€

Longueville is one of Ireland's finest country-house hotels, but for all its grandeur it is a friendly, unintimi-dating place. The main dining room, lined with portraits of previous Irish presidents, leads to a Victorian con-servatory, romantically candle-lit during the evening. A seven-course tasting menu is offered to whole par-ties, and it the best introduction to the chef's style. William O'Callaghan trained under Raymond Blanc, and the cooking is simple and well judged, the artistry in the clever combinations. Home-produced and local ingredients include home-smoked salmon and home-cured ham.

Prices are per person, for two courses, not including drinks:

€€€€	over 38 euros
€€€	28–38 euros
€€	20–28 euros
€	under 20 euros

Kinsale and Roaringwater Bay

Casino House
Coolmain Bay, Kilbrittain, Co. Cork;
tel: 023-884 9944; Thur–Tue D, L
Sun only, Nov, Jan–Mar, tel to confirm; €€€

This traditional farmhouse has been
stripped down and beautifully renovated as two simple but elegant dining
rooms, each with its own ante-room,
and colour theme. An international
concern, Kerrin from the Friesian
islands runs front of house with
warmth and flair, and her Croatian
husband Michael's imaginative
cooking and light touch have won
them many accolades. In summer try
his signature lobster risotto followed
by fruit sabayon.

Fishy Fishy Restaurant
Crowley's Pier, Kinsale; tel: 021-470
0415; www.fishyfishy.ie; L, D daily;
€€–€€€

One of Ireland's leading seafood restaurants occupies a substantial house
in the town park. In summer there is
a glamorous canopied area that feels
like the deck of a yacht. If you've never
tried real scampi made from freshly
caught jumbo prawns, now is your
chance. The salads are huge, with
the warm salad of seafood a lunch-
time favourite. Owner-chef Martin
Shanahan cooks only today's catch,
and does so with great panache, having
learnt his trade in San Francisco.

Max's Wine Bar
48 Main Street, Kinsale, Co. Cork;
tel: 021-477 2260; Wed–Mon, L D,
closed Nov–Mar; €€€

In a town replete with good restaurants, discerning locals invariably
mention Max's as one of the best. The
tiny, low-beamed room in a 400-year-
old town house has highly varnished
mahogany tables behind its cheerful
red-painted windowpanes. French
owner-chef Olivier Queva respects
the traditions of haute cuisine – try his
lightly seared pâté de foie gras – and
does great things with local seafood,
while his Irish wife provides the traditional welcome.

Bantry Bay

Bantry Bay Hotel
Wolfe Tone Square, Bantry; tel: 027-
50062; daily, B, L, D; €

The bar of this small Victorian hotel is
long and narrow, with restaurant tables
at the rear, but the place to sit, weather
permitting, is out on the square where
you can watch the world go by. The
menu is simple, but the food is carefully sourced: the open crab sandwich
is zingingly fresh, while the burgers are
home-made from local meat, and the
fish and chips are first-rate.

The Sheep's Head
Durrus; tel: 027-61109; L, D (tel to
confirm this) Nov–Mar; €€

A convivial pub in the centre of the
village, with a labyrinthine interior,

the Sheep's Head does a roaring trade in plates of simple, fortifying food for hungry walkers. At lunch time there are some good salad combinations, toasted sandwiches and panini, alongside more substantial daily specials, and in the evening steak or scampi and chips are popular options.

The Ring of Beara

Josie's Lakeview House

Cloghereen, Lauragh; tel: 064-668 3155; L, D, closed Nov-Feb; €–€€

The simple dining room is in a small conservatory extension with lovely views of the Glanmore Lake, nestling beneath the hills. Josie is a talented chef, who grew up in the area, and knows all the best suppliers of fresh fish and local meat. Try the trio of salmon, turbot and tiger prawns, or choose between a fillet steak or a rib eye. You can also just order a coffee and home-baked scone and enjoy the view.

Mulcahy's

30 Henry Street, Kenmare; tel: 064-664 2383; Mon–Sat, closed Tue–Wed, Oct–May; D €€€

When you're looking for a fancy restaurant, do what the locals do on this side of Beara, and head to Kenmare. Mulcahy's is a simple, low-key room with plate-glass windows, indicating its previous life as a pub. Bruce Mulcahy is one of the best owner-chefs in the business, having studied *sushi*-making

in Japan and learnt about fusion food in Thailand. The six-course tasting menu is a good introduction to his style, or try beef Carpaccio or Kerry lamb with a cep and carpaccio crust.

Killarney

Cellar One

The Ross Hotel, Town Centre, Killarney; tel: 064-663 1855; www.the ross.ie; daily, D; €€€

One of Killarney's landmark old hotels with lovely bow-fronted windows was recently given a major face-lift to emerge as a stunning boutique hotel, with leather seats in electric green counterpointed by shocking-pink cushions. The food in its dazzlingly dramatic Cellar One restaurant is the culinary equivalent of the decor, with a signature main course of tequila prawn and firecracker rice, and retro-style individual baked Alaska to follow.

Gaby's Seafood

27 High Street, Killarney; tel: 064-663 2519; D Wed–Sat, closed Jan–Feb; €€€€

Belgian owner-chef Gert Maes runs one of Ireland's finest seafood establishments in the town centre of Killarney. The decor is baronial in a continental style (lots of carved light wood and plush drapery), and there is a popular lower level at the front. Cooking is classic: the signature dish, lobster Gaby, is served with a cream and cognac sauce, or try the massive

Above from far left: coffee shop and bakery in Tralee; trendy décor at Cellar One, the restaurant in the landmark, now boutique, Ross Hotel *(centre and above)*.

seafood platter. There is also a selection of steaks and local lamb.

The Ring of Kerry

La Cascade

Sheen Falls Lodge, Kenmare; tel: 064-664 1600; www.sheenfalls lodge.ie; D daily; €€€€

In a luxury hotel just across the river from Kenmare town, the restaurant overlooks the floodlit tumbling waterfall from which it takes its name. An open fire crackles in the welcoming lobby, as your feet sink into thick-pile carpet. The menu consists of classic French cuisine, with main courses like fillet of turbot with cauliflower mousseline, or loin of lamb poached in olive oil, and a dazzling array of desserts, all impeccably served.

The Smuggler's Inn

Waterville, Co. Kerry; tel: 066-947 4330; www.the-smugglers-inn.com; daily Mar–Oct, L and D; €€–€€€

Generations of golfers, anglers and holiday-makers have eaten at this landmark cliff-top restaurant, right beside the famous championship links. In good weather you can eat outside at tables overlooking a long stretch of sandy beach, while the large conservatory area has an amazing panorama of sea and mountains. Owner-chef Henry Hunt cooks in a classic style, with an emphasis on seafood, Kerry lamb and excellent steaks. Lunch and early dinner offer especially good value.

The Dingle Peninsula

The Chart House

The Mall, Dingle; tel: 066-915 2255; daily June–Sept, Oct–May tel to confirm, D; €€€

The bright red half-door of Jim McCarthy's stone-built cottage restaurant is the first thing you see on arriving at Dingle, and it always lifts the spirits. Jim meets and greets visitors in the smart little bar. A favourite starter is local black pudding in filo pastry with apple and date chutney and hollandaise. Pork is served with brandied apples, pan-fried brill with smoked bacon and rocket. Desserts such as sticky maple and macadamia-nut pudding with butterscotch sauce are highlights.

Doyle's Seafood Bar

5 John Street, Dingle; tel: 066-915 1174; D Mon–Sat; €€

Originally a tiny pub, dating from 1790, today Doyle's is a restaurant famed for its seafood (although still tiny). The stone floor, kitchen range and wooden bar have been retained, creating an atmospheric, old-world-style interior. Doyle's was one of the first restaurants to open in Dingle, and is untainted by trends, serving simply prepared local seafood and bistro classics including beef and Guinness stew, and roast rack of Kerry mountain lamb. Desserts are traditional too, and there's a good farmhouse cheese platter.

Tralee and North Kerry

Kate Browne's Pub

Ardfert, Co. Kerry; tel: 066-713 4055; daily, L, D; €–€€

This traditional thatched cottage with rough-cast walls stands at the entrance to a pretty country village. Kate Browne's is one of the best-known pub-restaurants in County Kerry. As on the outside, the interior is also cottage-like, with long rough-hewn tables, and *sugán* (straw-seated) chairs. The menu features old reliable dishes, such as seafood chowder, baked mussels, steaks and a few lighter options, but don't imagine the food is less interesting as a result; the seafood is as fresh as it comes, and the steaks are renowned.

Samuel Restaurant

Grand Hotel, Denny Street, Tralee; tel: 066-712 1499; www.grandhotel tralee.com; daily, B, L, D; €–€€

Tralee has never had a fine-dining scene, but this hotel-restaurant (known as 'Samuels') is a reliable substitute, and a popular spot with locals for special occasions. Chandeliers hang above wood-panelled walls, and the staff are friendly and attentive. The food is standard fare – roast meat, steaks and fresh seafood – prepared by chef Pat Moynihan from the finest local suppliers. Choose between à la carte or table d'hôte at dinner. If you're lucky, there will also be music in the bar afterwards.

Bunratty, Limerick and Adare

Aubars Bar Bistro

49–50 Thomas Street, Limerick; tel: 061-317 572; www.aubar.com; daily, L, D; €

A city-centre bar on a pedestrianised street has been converted into this dramatically lit metropolitan hang-out, which has several levels and heated outdoor tables. A lively spot, popular with Limerick's younger crowd, it has a range of menus, and offers 10 wines by the glass. Rib-eye steak with Béarnaise sauce, rocket and chunky chips, or tiger prawn stir-fry with pak choi and egg noodles are typical main courses. The menu caters well for vegetarians.

The Wild Geese

Rose Cottage, Main Street, Adare; tel: 061-396 451; www.thewild geese.com; Tue–Sat D, Sun L and D; €–€€€

Occupying one of Adare's thatched cottages, this is a serious restaurant, with a well-travelled owner-chef offering excellent modern Irish cuisine. Tables are dressed in white napery, and the décor is like that of a Victorian doll's house. The menu is luxurious, with a wide choice. Pan-seared scallops are served on a potato pancake, while roast rack of Adare lamb comes with herby potato gratin and rosemary *jus*. All the desserts are made on the premises: the best bet is to share a two-person dessert plate.

Above from far left: storing the pride of the Irish; dinner at La Cascade; exterior of the Smuggler's Inn.

CREDITS

Insight Step by Step Cork and Southwest Ireland
Written by: Alannah Hopkin
Series Editor: Clare Peel
Editor: Maria Lord
Map Production: APA Cartography Department
Picture Manager: Steven Lawrence
Art Editor: Richard Cooke
Photography: APA/Kevin Cummings 2BM, 2BR, 2MM, 5MT, 6ML, 6MR, 7BL, 7TL, 7TR, 9BR, 9ML, 9MM, 12TL, 15T, 16–17, 17MT, 20B, 20M, 28BR, 28ML, 30, 31B, 31M, 31T, 32–3, 32B, 32TL, 33TR, 34B, 34M, 35TR, 40–1, 40TL, 41TL, 48–9, 48TL, 49TR, 55TR, 60, 62–3, 62M, 62TL, 63TR, 64, 65B, 65M, 68, 69B, 70–1, 70B, 70T, 71TR, 78B, 78M, 84BL, 86, 91, 91TL, 93TR, 94, 104TL, 106TL; APA/Glyn Genin 2MR, 2BL, 2MR, 4MB, 4T, 6BL, 9–10, 9BL, 9BM, 9MR, 10–11, 11B, 11MB, 11TR, 12–13, 13M, 13TR, 19B, 23T, 28-29, 28BM, 28MM, 32M, 34–5, 34TL, 36–7, 37B, 38–9, 38TL, 39, 43, 43B, 43M, 46–7, 46TL, 50, 51, 52–3, 52B, 52TL, 53M, 54TL, 55MB, 65T, 66TL, 70M, 72B, 72M, 72T, 76B, 74M, 74TL, 76T, 77, 78TL, 80, 81M, 81T, 84–5, 84BM, 84MM, 84MR, 87, 88TL, 90, 91B, 92–3, 95, 103; APA/Corrie Wingate 2–3, 4MT, 13B, 14, 15B, 15MB, 17B, 17TR, 19MB. 19MT, 82–3, 82B, 82M, 82TL, 83TR, 84TL; FLICKR/Stig Anderson 75TR; Ballyhoura 48B, Julie Berlin 62B; 48M; Big Mick 21; Bernd Bragelman 7BR, 89T; Natale Carioni 58–9; Falco500 6TL; Corey Harmon 58M; Dan Heatherley 61M; Liam Hughes 4M, 47TR; Deanna Keahey 70; Jim Linwood 74–5; Paul O'Mahoney 24, 25T, 78–9, 79TR, 88-89; Mozzercork 44–5, 44TL; Anthony Patterson 57M, 61B; L Pycock 11MT; Pam Ramsay 66B, 66M, 76B; Shadowgate 16TL, 18, 19T; Dale Smith 66–7; Technohippybiker 10TL, Padraig Woods 45TR; iStockphoto/7MR, 22TL, 24B, 24M, 56, 58TL, 61T; Photolibrary/26, 27, 54–5, 54B, 59TR, 67TR; Rex Features/25T; Superstock/4B; Café Paradiso 102; Cascade Hotel 106–7; Cellar One 104–5, 105TR; Hayfield Manor 28MR, 96, 97; The Maritime Bantry Bay 99TR; Parksanilla Hotel 100–1, 100TL; Richmond Gardens 98TL; Smuggles Inn 107TR.
Front Cover: main image: 4Corners; inset images: iStockphoto.
Printed by: CTPS-China.

© 2011 APA Publications GmbH & Co. Verlag KG (Singapore branch)

All rights reserved

First Edition 2011

No part of this book may be reproduced, stored in a retrieval system or transmitted in any form or by any means (electronic, mechanical, photocopying, recording or otherwise), without prior written permission of APA Publications. Brief text quotations with use of photographs are exempted for book review purposes only. Information has been obtained from sources believed to be reliable, but its accuracy and completeness, and the opinions based thereon, are not guaranteed.

Although Insight Guides and the authors of this book have taken all reasonable care in preparing it, we make no warranty about the accuracy or completeness of its content, and, to the maximum extent permitted, disclaim all liability arising from its use.

CONTACTING THE EDITORS

We would appreciate it if readers would alert us to errors or outdated information by writing to us at insight@apaguide.co.uk or APA Publications, PO Box 7910, London SE1 1WE, UK.

www.insightguides.com

DISTRIBUTION

Worldwide
**APA Publications GmbH & Co. Verlag KG
(Singapore branch)**
7030 Ang Mo Kio Ave 5
08-65 Northstar @ AMK, Singapore 569880
Email: apasin@singnet.com.sg

UK and Ireland
GeoCenter International Ltd
Meridian House, Churchill Way West
Basingstoke, Hampshire RG21 6YR
Email: sales@geocenter.co.uk

US
Ingram Publisher Services
One Ingram Blvd, PO Box 3006
La Vergne, TN 37086-1986
Email: customer.service@ingrampublisher
services.com

Australia
Universal Publishers
1 Waterloo Road
Macquarie Park
NSW 2113
Email: sales@universalpublishers.com.au

New Zealand
Hema Maps New Zealand Ltd (HNZ)
Unit 2
10 Cryers Road
East Tamaki
Auckland 2013
Email: sales.hema@clear.net.nz

INDEX

A

accommodation 96–101
Adare 83
    Adare Manor 83
    Augustinian friary 83
    Heritage Centre 83
    Trinitarian priory 83
Adrigole 60–1, 63
age restrictions 86
airports 93
Allihies 62–3
    Copper Mine Museum 62–3
angling 22–3, 66–7
Annascaul 74
    South Pole Inn 74
Annes Grove Garden 49
architecture 11–12
Ardfert 78

Ardgroom 63
    Stone Circle 62
art galleries 31–2, 35, 83

B

Ballybeg Augustinian Friary 49
Ballybunion 79
    Seaweed Baths 79
Ballycotton 40–1
Ballydehob 55
Ballydonegan 62
Ballyduff 78
    Ratoo Round Tower 78
Ballyferriter 75
Ballyhooly 48
Ballymaloe Cookery School and Gardens 15, 40–1
Ballymaloe House 14–15, 40

Baltimore 55
Banna Strand 78
Bantry Bay 56–9
    Ballylickey 59
    Bantry House and Gardens 58–9
    Garinish Island 59
    Glengarriff 59
    Glengarriff Woods Nature Reserve 59
    town 59
Beara Way, the 60
beehive huts 75
Bere Island 61
Blackwater Valley 46–9
Blarney 42–3
    Blarney Castle 42–3
    Blarney Stone 43
Blasket Islands 74
    Great Blasket, the 74

Bowen, Elizabeth 24, 49
Bridgetown Priory 48
Brunel, Isambard Kingdom
    37
budgeting 86
Bunratty 80
    Castle 80
    Folk Park 80
buses 94
Buttevant 49

C

Cahirciveen 69
    Gallery One 69
    O'Connell Memorial
        Church 69
    Old Barracks 69
    tourist information 69
    White Strand Beach 69
Camp, Dingle Peninsula 76
Cape Clear 55
car hire 95
carbon-offsetting 89
Carrigadrohid Castle 43–4
Casement, Roger 78
cash machines 91
Castle Hyde 48
Castlemaine 73
Castletownbere 60, 61
    McCarthy's Bar 60, 61
Castletownroche 48–9
Charles Fort 50
children 86
climate 12
Clonakilty 53
clothing 87
Cobh 36, 37–9
    Lusitania Memorial 38
    Old Yacht Club 38
    Queenstown Story 38
    St Colman's Cathedral 39
    Titanic Trail 39
Conor Pass 76
consulates 88
Coomakista Pass 71

Cork City 30–5
    city centre 30–2
    Cornmarket Street Bridge
        32
    Cork City Gaol and Radio
        Museum 35
    Cork Public Museum 35
    Crawford Municipal Art
        Gallery 31–2
    English Market 15,
        30–1
    Fitzgerald Park 35
    Grand Parade 30
    Mardyke Walk 35
    Opera House 32
    Paul Street 31
    St Fin Barre's Cathedral 34
    St Patrick Street 31
    Shandon, *see Shandon, p.112*
    tourist information 30
    University College 34–5
Cork Harbour 36–9
crafts 19, 33, 40, 69
credit cards 91
crime and safety 87
crystal 19
currency 91
customs 87
cycling 23

D

dance 20
Derreen Garden 63
Derreenataggart Stone Circle
    62
Derrynane House and
    National Park 71
Dingle 74–5
Dingle Bay 68–9
    Cahirciveen 69
    Glenbeigh 69
    Kerry Bog Village Museum
        68–9
    Killorglin 68–9
    Rossbeigh 69

Dingle Peninsula 73–6
disabled travellers 87–8
Doneraile Park 49
drinks 17
driving 94–5
Drombeg Stone Circle 53
Dunbeg Promontory Fort 74
Dunboy 61–2
    Dunboy House 62
Dunquin 75
    Dunquin Pier 75
Durrus 56, 58
Dzogchen Beara Buddhist
    Retreat Centre 62, 99

E

economy 13
electricity 88
embassies 88
emergencies 88
etiquette 88
Eyeries 63

F

Fahan 75
Farrell, J.G. 58
Fastnet Rock Lighthouse 54
Fermoy 47
festivals 21
film 24
food and drink 14–17, 102–7
food shops 19
Fota Island 37
    Fota House, Gardens and
        Arboretum 37
    Fota Wildlife Park 37
Future Forests 45

G

Gaelic Games 22
Gallarus Oratory 75, 76
Gallí, Beth 30
Gap of Dunloe 67

Garryvue **41**
gay and lesbian issues
    89
Gearagh, the **44**
geography **10–11**
Gibbings, Robert **24**, **44**
Glandore **53–4**
Glenbeg Lough **63**
golf **22**, **66**, **71**, **83**
Gougane Barra **45**
Great Blasket, the **75**
    Great Blasket Centre **75**
green issues **89**

H

Hag of Beara **62**, **63**
health **89**
Healy Pass, the **63**
Heritage Card **86**
history **11–12**, **26–7**
holidays **90**
horse riding **23**
hospitals **90**
hotels **96–101**
Hungry Hill **60–1**

I

Inch **73–4**
Inchigeelagh **44**
Inniscarra **43**
Inniscarra Lake **43**
internet **90**

J

jaunting cars **64**, **66**

K

Kenmare village **72**
    Heritage Centre **72**
Kenmare Bay **63**
Kenmare River **72**
Kerry cows **65**

Killarney National Park **64–7**
    Dunloe Castle **66–7**
    Gap of Dunloe **67**
    Golf and Fishing Club **66**
    Innisfallen Island **66**
    Kate Kearney's Cottage **67**
    Ladies' View **64**
    Muckross House and Park
        65
    Muckross Road **66**
    Ross Castle **66**
    Torc Waterfall **64**
    walks **65**
Kilcatherine **63**
Kilcrohane **58**
Kilmakillogue Harbour **63**
Kilmalkedar Church **76**
Kinsale **50–2**
    Compass Hill **52**
    Court House **51**
    Desmond Castle **51**
    Green Lane **52**
    International Museum of
        Wine **51–2**
    Kinsale Museum **51**
    Main Street **52**
    Mall **52**
    Municipal Hall **52**
    Old Head of Kinsale **50**
    Pier Head **52**
    Pier Road **52**
    St John's Hill **52**
    St Multose **51**
    Southwell Gift Houses **52**
    tourist information **52**

L

Labbacallee **47–8**
Megalithic Wedge Tomb
    47–8
Lee Valley **43–5**
lighthouses **54**, **55**, **58**
Limerick **81–3**
    Arthur's Quay **81**
    City Museum **82**

Crescent, the **82**
Georgian House and
    Garden **82**
Hunt Museum **81**
King John's Castle **82**
Limerick City Gallery of
    Art **83**
Pery Square **82**
riverside footpath **82**
St Mary's Cathedral **81**
tourist information **81**
university **81**
Lismore **46–7**
    Castle **46–7**
    Castle Gardens and
        Art Gallery **47**
    Heritage Centre **46**
    St Carthage's Cathedral **47**
Listowel **79**
    Castle **79**
    St John's Church **79**
    Writers' Week **79**
literary heritage **24–5**
local customs **13**

M

Maharees, the **23**
Mallow **49**
    Longueville House **49**
    Mallow Castle **49**
maps **90**
markets **15**, **18**,
    30–1, **38**
media **91**
Midleton **38**, **39–41**
    Old Midleton Distillery **40**
Mizen Head Visitor Centre
    55
mobile phones **92**
money **91**
music venues **20–1**

N

newpapers **91**

O

O'Connell, Daniel 69, 71, 72
Oceanworld Mara Beo
    Aquarium 75
Ogham Stones 76
opening times 19, 90

P

Pass of Keimaneigh 45
passports 95
pharmacies 90
police 91
politics 13
population 13–14
Portmagee 70
postal service 91–2
potato famine 12, 54
public holidays 90
public transport 94
pubs 17

R

railways 94
religion 92
restaurants 102–7
Ring of Beara 60
Ring of Kerry 68–72
River Laune 66–7
Riverdance 48
Roaringwater Bay 54–5
Ross Castle 66
Rosscarbery 53

S

St Finbar's Day 45
Schull 55
Seven Heads Walk 50
Shanagarry 40–1
    Design Centre 40
    Shanagarry House 40–1
Shandon, Cork 32–4
    Butter Exchange 33

Cork Bitter Museum 33
Cork Vision Centre 34
Firkin Crane 33
Pope's Quay 32–3
St Anne's Shandon 33–4
St Mary's Dominican
    Church 32–3
Shandon Craft Centre 33
Shandon Street 34
Sheep's Head 56–8
    Ahakista 57
    Air India Memorial 56–7
    Durrus 56
    Goat's Path 58
    Kilcrohane 58
    Kilnaruane Pillar Stone 58
    Rossnacaheragh Stone
        Circle 57
    St James Church of Ireland
        56
    Sheep's Head Lighthouse 58
    Sheep's Head Way 56
Sherkin Island 55
shopping 18–19
Skellig Rocks 71
    Skellig Experience Visitor
        Centre 71
Skibbereen 54
    Heritage Centre 54
Slea Head 74, 75
smoking 92
Sneem 72
    Garden of the Senses 72
    Parknasilla Hotel 72
Spenser, Edmund 24, 49
sports 22–3
stone circles 26, 53,
    57, 62
surfing 23

T

taxis 94
telephones 92
television and radio 91
theatre 20

time zones 92
Timoleague 50, 52–3
    Timoleague Abbey 53
tipping 91
Titanic, the 37, 38, 39
toilets 93
tourist information 93
Tralee 77
    Kerry County Museum 77
transport 93–5

U

University College, Cork
    34–5
    Glucksman Gallery 35
    Honan Chapel 35
    Visitor Centre 35

V

Valentia Island 70
    Glanleam Subtropical
        Gardens 70
    ferries 70, 93
    Knightstown 70
Ventry 74
visas 95

W

walking 23
Waterville 71
websites 95
weights and measures 95
Whiddy Island 57
whiskey 17, 40

Y

Youghal 41
    Clock Tower 41
    Heritage Centre 41
    Myrtle Grove 41
    St Mary's Collegiate
        Church 41

Tours

1 Cork City   p31

2 Cork Harbour and East Cork   p38-9

3 Blarney Castle and the Lee Valley   p44-5

4 Blackwater Valley and North Cork   p48

5 Kinsale and Roaringwater Bay   p51 & 52

6 Bantry Bay   p57

7 The Ring of Beara   p61

8 Killarney   p65

9 The Ring of Kerry   p69

10 The Dingle Peninsula   p73

11 Tralee and North Kerry   p78

12 Bunratty, Limerick and Adare   p80 & 82